UNEMPLOYMENT, IDLE CAPACITY, AND THE EVALUATION OF PUBLIC EXPENDITURES: NATIONAL AND REGIONAL ANALYSES

UNEMPLOYMENT, IDLE CAPACITY, AND THE EVALUATION OF PUBLIC EXPENDITURES:

NATIONAL AND REGIONAL ANALYSES

ROBERT H. HAVEMAN

JOHN V. KRUTILLA

with the assistance of

ROBERT M. STEINBERG

PUBLISHED FOR RESOURCES FOR THE FUTURE, INC.
BY THE JOHNS HOPKINS PRESS, BALTIMORE, MARYLAND

PREFACE

In recent decades there has been a marked increase in the use of public expenditure criteria in both the process of choosing among alternative public expenditures and the process of designing public works projects. In applying these criteria, analysts of public expenditures have conventionally assumed full employment. This assumption is acknowledged to be essential if market cost and price data are to reflect their real counterparts and serve effectively in the comparison of social costs and benefits. Having made this assumption, the analyst finds his case greatly weakened if the economy fails to operate at full employment. Indeed, under conditions of substantial unemployment the nominal or market cost-price data lose normative significance and are of limited aid in evaluating public expenditure alternatives.

While the existence of unemployment long has been recognized as a problem for benefit-cost analysis, its empirical solution, which requires the estimation of appropriate benefit and cost adjustments under various conditions of unemployment, has not been possible until recently. A short time ago, however, the new interindustry relations matrix with a more disaggregated treatment of the construction sector prepared by the Office of Business Economics of the U.S. Department of Commerce became available. This has removed one of the major obstacles to undertaking such a study as a manageable research effort. In addition, the Bureau of Labor Statistics has completed its industry-occupation relations matrix, which permits the estimation of the indirect off-site demands on each of several occupational categories in the construction of any major undertaking, public or private. These two new sources of data have enabled the development of models which trace the final bill of goods for construction to the factor sources which supply the primary inputs to public expenditures of any sort. In Chapters II and III of this volume, these models are presented and statistically implemented.

Through a comparison of the occupational labor demands and rates of unemployment by occupation, relationships can be developed to estimate the percentage of the labor required for the construction of public projects which will be drawn from the idle pool. Industrial output demands and estimates of capacity utilization by industry serve as the basis for developing estimates of the percentage of capital facilities used which were idle. These estimates and the procedures for obtaining them are shown in Chapter IV.

In this study then, we have sought to begin evaluating the opportunity cost of public expenditures in periods of less than full employment by analyzing one type—water resource development—among the whole range of public expenditures. We believe that the form of analysis presented here is now a feasible undertaking for the entire gamut of public expenditure programs and urge that it be undertaken.

This study has been supported by The Brookings Institution and Resources for the Future. The authors are indebted to their colleagues at RFF and Grinnell College for stimulation and assistance given during several seminar sessions over the course of the work on this problem. The authors are particularly indebted to Robert M. Steinberg, without whose assistance in programming the computer operations and numerous useful suggestions in other respects, the study could not have been successfully completed. Appendices 5, 6, and 9 are largely his work. Helpful criticism was received from Blair T. Bower, Michael F. Brewer, Robert K. Davis, J. Charles Headley, Charles W. Howe, Allen V. Kneese, Jack L. Knetsch, Robert C. Lind, and George J. Stolnitz during the period that both authors were engaged in this study at Resources for the Future. Acknowledgment is due William Capron of The Brookings Institution for a review and helpful comments on an earlier draft of the study. Ronald J. Wonnacott, John Cumberland, and Otto Eckstein also were particularly helpful in reviewing the manuscript, and their numerous constructive criticisms have gone far to strengthen portions of the study. Among other reviewers to whom we are indebted are A. Myrick Freeman III, William Miernyk, Paul Mlotok, John Peterson, and Ralph Turvey.

In addition to reviewing the manuscript, Norman Frumkin, Robert Summers, Claiborne Ball, and Harry Greenspan were most helpful in making data available and providing technical assistance. In this latter capacity, the help of James Walker, Herman Rothberg, Albert Walderhaug, and Roland Murray is also gratefully acknowledged.

Finally, the expert editing by Virginia Parker and art work by Clare and Frank Ford are gratefully acknowledged.

March 20, 1968   ROBERT H. HAVEMAN and JOHN V. KRUTILLA

CONTENTS

APPENDICES

LIST OF TABLES

APPENDIX TABLES

LIST OF FIGURES

APPENDIX FIGURES

UNEMPLOYMENT, IDLE CAPACITY, AND THE EVALUATION OF PUBLIC EXPENDITURES: NATIONAL AND REGIONAL ANALYSES

THE SOCIAL COST OF PUBLIC INVESTMENT
IN A LESS THAN FULLY EMPLOYED ECONOMY

1

OVER THE PAST TWO DECADES the expenditure side of the U.S. economy's public sector has been studied intensively. An increasing number of monographs and articles has dealt with the conceptual underpinning and empirical estimation of benefits and costs of public works and other public investment programs.[1] A great deal of effort and ingenuity has been devoted to identifying and estimating both marketable and nonmarketable benefits from public programs; somewhat less attention has been given to the opportunity cost of public expenditures. Aside from the rather extensive discussion of the opportunity cost of capital diverted from the private sector for public programs,[2] it has been assumed that the relevant markets reflect with sufficient accuracy the costs of factor services and intermediate goods employed by the public sector. The presumption has been that if the market can be assumed ordinarily to function reasonably well and the economy is fully employed, wage rates and the prices of material and equipment accurately reflect the opportunity cost of resources used in the economy.[3]

Use of factor market prices as the opportunity cost of resources assumes that both labor mobility and effective demand are sufficient to result in a fully employed economy. While it is generally recognized that these conditions are not universally met, many economists have held that the assumption of full employment in criteria for public expenditures has general utility. Thus, Otto Eckstein argues that adjustments to the benefits or costs of investments in areas of chronically high unemployment would retard the development of the required mobility for efficient performance of the labor market, and suggests that such adjustments not be made.[4] He concedes, however, that if severe unemployment is experienced, benefits and costs should be recalculated to allow for the re-

[1] See A. R. Prest and R. Turvey, "Cost-Benefit Analysis: A Survey," *The Economic Journal*, Vol. 75 (December 1965), pp. 683–735, for a review of the literature and an extensive bibliography on the subject.
[2] For a review of a large part of this discussion, see Otto Eckstein, "A Survey of the Theory of Public Expenditure Criteria," *Public Finances: Needs, Sources and Utilization*, Conference of the Universities-National Bureau Committee for Economic Research (Princeton: Princeton University Press, 1961).
[3] Otto Eckstein, *Water Resources Development, The Economics of Project Evaluation* (Cambridge: Harvard University Press, 1958), p. 29.
[4] *Ibid.*, pp. 32–35.

1

duction in social costs when idle factors are employed. The position seems to be that all projects should be evaluated by a uniform criterion at the time the project is planned, and that benefit and cost adjustments to reflect low levels of employment should be made as a separate calculation when a decision is taken to build during a period of low employment. This seems also to be the position taken by McKean[5] as well as by Hirshleifer, De Haven, and Milliman.[6]

Other analysts, however, appear somewhat more amenable to the idea of adjusting market prices when the opportunity costs of factors diverge from nominal or market costs.[7] The problem of the unemployed in chronically depressed areas is a case in point. One often hears the argument that in some chronically depressed areas—such as Appalachia, the Ozarks, and the Sangre de Cristo mountain communities in the United States—the indigenous labor force becomes "locked in" and for all practical purposes is immobile. While the real estate market in such areas is depressed if not nonexistent, the available living accommodations, although submarginal, do offer shelter of a kind. Also a minimum subsistence is extracted from the environment. Because movement out of the region implies securing new living accommodations which would exceed the itinerant's financial resources, the fixed assets of the indigent tend to freeze him in the depressed area.[8] The continued failure of conditions to improve may not force the unemployed to move out of the depressed area. In fact, the passage of time may render the indigenous labor force less capable of meeting the requirements of active labor markets.[9] In these cases, the employment of the local labor force in public projects may involve little opportunity cost, and yet have little adverse effect on the development of increased labor mobility.

Another type of unemployment situation has not been dealt with explicitly in the literature on public expenditures. This is exemplified by

[5] Roland McKean, *Efficiency in Government Through Systems Analysis* (New York: John Wiley and Sons, 1958), pp. 160–62.
[6] Jack Hirshleifer, James C. De Haven, and Jerome W. Milliman, *Water Supply: Economics, Technology and Policy* (Chicago: University of Chicago Press, 1960), pp. 130–31.
[7] See for example, Maynard M. Hufschmidt, John Krutilla, and Julius Margolis, Report of Panel of Consultants to the Bureau of the Budget, *Standards and Criteria for Formulating and Evaluating Federal Water Resources Development* (Washington, June 30, 1961), pp. 19, 31–33; Alan T. Peacock and D. J. Robertson, *Public Expenditure and Appraisal Control* (Edinburgh: Oliver and Boyd, 1963), p. 6; and, particularly, Stephen A. Marglin in Arthur Maass, *et al., Design of Water-Resource Systems* (Cambridge: Harvard University Press, 1962), pp. 50–51.
[8] For a discussion of the effect of the fixity of assets on labor mobility, see Glenn L. Johnson, "Supply Functions, Some Facts and Notions," in Earl O. Heady *et al., Agricultural Adjustment Problems in a Growing Economy* (Ames: Iowa State University Press, 1958), Chap. IV.
[9] For an analysis of this problem, see Rufus B. Hughes, "Interregional Income Differences: Self Perpetuation," *Southern Economic Journal*, Vol. 28 (July 1961), pp. 41–45.

the employment history of the U. S. economy from 1957 until the tax cut of 1964 and the expanded involvement in the war in Southeast Asia. In spite of high and growing levels of income and employment, additions to the labor force tended to exceed the additional employment opportunities created by the economy's rate of growth. A question arises whether such a condition poses a different kind of problem from that previously discussed. To what extent was the disparity between the rate of growth of employment opportunities and the rate of growth of the labor force caused by structural elements? To what extent did it result from the failure of the national government to employ decisively the measures at its command for stimulating effective demand? If the latter, is there assurance that such a situation will not again prevail over extended periods of time? In either event, although unemployment is neither regionally specific and chronic nor of depression severity, the duration and universal incidence of idle resources appear to require that investments in the public sector be evaluated with observed costs adjusted for the difference between market and opportunity values.

Much the same analytic framework and data are required whether one decides to use full employment as the criterion in planning and project evaluation, reserving the option to recalculate benefits and costs if employment conditions warrant, or decides to adjust costs when the project is first evaluated.[10] In either case, data are required on the demand made on the several sectors of the economy supplying construction inputs to the project, and the employment performance in such sectors. Other required knowledge includes the occupational skills demanded by various types of public works projects, both at the construction site and in the industrial sectors supplying material and equipment for the project, and the unemployment situation in these occupational categories. Also, there are such questions as these: Does the project demand the kind of skills available in the depressed areas or required by the depressed industrial sectors? Or can the project use unskilled labor? How significant a proportion of the project costs are represented by outlays for factor services which would otherwise remain idle? Are the required cost adjustments dependent on the region within which the projects are undertaken? Are the adjustments for projects undertaken in areas of chronic labor surplus different from the required adjustment for projects undertaken during a period of moderate and more or less uniform national unemployment? How should the adjustment to nominal costs be varied, if at all, to take account of a rate of unemployment ranging from moderate to severe?

[10] While the information regarding project inputs and their opportunity costs will be the same, the former position does not require the forecasting of future unemployment rates by occupation and industry. This is a serious problem for public works projects requiring a long construction period—for example, large multiple-purpose water resource projects. It is not a problem in many categories of water development and other public works undertakings having a construction period measured in months rather than years.

Similarly, questions regarding the cost of using idle industrial capacity arise. Is there an opportunity cost if the capacity otherwise would be idle during the period of project construction? Does the storability of such factor services require distinction between the treatment of labor and capital goods in assessing opportunity costs during the relevant interval?

In this study we adopt the following position. We recognize that idle industrial capacity does not yield a return on invested capital. Thus, we will not include any rate of return over costs in the price of goods or services from industrial sectors operating below capacity.[11] Since the services of durable capital goods can be claimed at some future time if not yielded in the present, the depreciation chargeable to the use of capital equipment is considered to be a true opportunity cost. Consequently, while the unemployed services of labor are perishable, and thus lost if not productively employed during an interval, only the rate of return on capital can be regarded as lost for the period in which capital equipment lies idle.[12]

Our objective is to estimate the divergence between nominal market values and true opportunity values involving public water resource investments. To this end, in Chapter II we address the question as though unemployment is more or less uniformly distributed across the nation, and employ a model of the economy which yields, without regional differentiation, estimates of the pattern of industrial and labor demands imposed by public project construction. In Chapter III, we elaborate the analysis by introducing regional dimensions of employment and output demands imposed by project construction. In Chapter IV, we estimate the extent to which nominal or market prices of factors require adjustments when evaluating public works under conditions of both (1) uniform national unemployment and (2) specific conditions of disparate regional unemployment patterns. Before proceeding with this analysis, we briefly review the national employment performance both of labor by occupational groups and capital by industry sectors in the postwar economy of the United States.

POSTWAR EMPLOYMENT IN THE U.S. ECONOMY

During the nineteen years of the postwar period (1947–65), employment in the United States has been consistently high and rising. Employ-

---

[11] This position is consistent with the viewpoint of Hufschmidt, Krutilla, and Margolis, *op. cit.*, p. 19.

[12] For very long periods of idleness, of course, technological obsolescence would appear as a cost no less real than capital consumption through wear. Our estimates of the divergence of opportunity costs from nominal costs, therefore, are the more conservative of the two possible positions.

FIGURE 1. POSTWAR EMPLOYMENT OF CIVILIAN LABOR FORCE, 1947–65

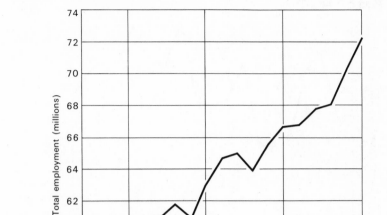

Source: U.S. Department of Labor, Manpower Administration, *Statistical Tables on Manpower: A Reprint from the 1966 Manpower Report* (Washington, 1966), Table A–1, p. 153.

ment receded from levels previously attained only in the years 1949, 1954, and 1958 (see Figure 1). At all other times, both employment and income were rising. Significantly, however, some of the years of high and rising employment experienced more than frictional unemployment. In the postwar period, unemployment rates of the civilian labor force were below 4 per cent in only five of the nineteen years (1947, 1948, 1951, 1952, and 1953, as shown in Figure 2). In all other years of high and rising employment, the unemployment rates were significantly above 4 per cent. In fact, during the twelve years following the termination of hostilities in Korea (1954–65)—or for the entire period between the Korean War and the U.S. military involvement in Vietnam—the unemployment rate remained consistently over 4 per cent.

However, average unemployment rates for the total civilian labor force may not be relevant in estimating the opportunity cost of idle resources employed by public projects. Substantial variation from the national unemployment rate might be expected for different types of projects. If the extreme values tend to be concentrated—or absent from —the industrial and occupational sectors from which the public project draws, the implications for cost adjustments will differ accordingly.

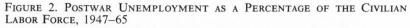

FIGURE 2. POSTWAR UNEMPLOYMENT AS A PERCENTAGE OF THE CIVILIAN
LABOR FORCE, 1947–65

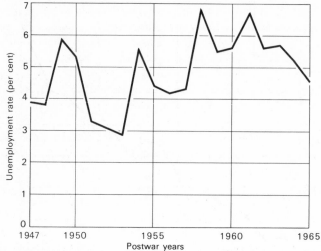

Source: U.S. Department of Labor, Manpower Administration, *Statistical Tables
on Manpower: A Reprint from the 1966 Manpower Report* (Washington, 1966),
Table A–1, p. 153.

Our study deals with construction in twelve categories covering all
types of water resource development projects, as follows:

Large earth fill dams	Powerhouse construction
Small earth fill dams	Medium concrete dams
Local flood protection	Lock and concrete dams
Pile dikes	Large multiple-purpose projects
Levees	Dredging
Revetments	Miscellaneous (all other types)

Water resource projects tend to make the heaviest demands on roughly
twenty industrial groups and a like number of occupational groups. The
unemployment data for the industrial groups important to project construction are shown in Table 1; the unemployment rates for the selected
occupational skills which figure most prominently in the projects are
shown in Table 2.[13] The employment performance in both breakdowns
is marked by the expected variation from average rates for the economy
as a whole.

The data from 1957 through 1964, the period for which detailed industrial breakdowns are available, are revealing. Assuming that unemployment rates of 4 per cent or more have implications for estimating

[13] Detailed breakdowns of industrial and occupational demands imposed by the
construction of water resource projects are shown in Tables 10A–2 and 10A–3 of
Appendix 10.

the opportunity costs of resource use, we notice that over half of the industrial groups in Table 1 show unemployment rates consistently above the standard. While only one group (finance, insurance, and real estate) shows an unemployment rate consistently below 4 per cent, there are inconsistent patterns, sometimes above and sometimes below the 4 per cent rate, in a number of the groups.

Does the unemployment rate by industrial groups give the best measure of the degree to which a pool of idle resources exists? We can assume that there is considerable labor mobility among industrial sectors, but not among occupational groups. If so, unemployment data by occupational groups combined with data on excess capacity by industrial groups will be more directly relevant for estimating the real costs of project construction when there exists some resource idleness.

The unemployment history by selected occupations summarized in Table 2 shows that over the eight-year period from 1957 through 1964, a considerable number of occupational groups experienced unemployment rates high enough to imply a divergence between market and opportunity costs. Eight of the total number registered unemployment rates consistently above 4 per cent. On the other hand, five of the groups most pertinent to water resource project construction had unemployment rates

Table 1. Unemployment Rates: U.S. Average and by Industry Groups Pertinent to Water Resource Projects, 1957–64 (unemployed as per cent of civilian labor force)

Industry group	1957	1958	1959	1960	1961	1962	1963	1964
U.S. average	4.3	6.8	5.5	5.6	6.7	5.6	5.7	5.2
Construction	9.8	13.7	12.0	12.2	14.1	12.0	11.9	9.9
Durable goods manufacturing	4.9	10.5	6.1	6.3	8.4	5.7	5.4	4.7
Lumber & wood products	8.5	11.6	8.7	9.1	11.1	8.4	8.4	8.8
Stone, clay, & glass products	5.1	8.7	5.3	6.0	8.1	6.4	6.3	4.9
Primary metal industries	3.6	11.4	5.3	7.8	10.9	7.0	4.3	2.8
Fabricated metal products	4.9	9.1	6.5	6.1	6.7	5.4	5.6	4.8
Machinery, except electrical	3.4	9.0	4.3	4.7	6.4	3.7	4.1	3.0
Electrical machinery	4.5	8.7	5.4	5.0	6.9	5.0	5.7	5.0
Transportation equipment	5.3	13.2	7.1	6.9	10.0	6.0	4.4	4.1
Automobiles only	6.9	21.3	10.1	8.4	13.9	6.1	3.7	3.4
Nondurable goods manufacturing	5.3	7.6	5.9	6.8	6.7	5.9	6.0	5.3
Chemicals & allied products	3.1	5.1	3.6	3.3	3.3	3.3	3.3	2.6
Other nondurable goods[a]	4.2	6.3	4.6	5.2	5.9	4.9	5.2	4.7
Transportation & public utilities	3.1	5.6	4.2	4.3	5.1	3.9	3.9	3.3
Railroads & railway express	3.7	9.8	5.0	5.2	6.8	5.2	4.3	3.5
Other transportation	4.0	6.3	5.8	5.7	6.5	4.8	5.4	4.5
Wholesale & retail trade	4.5	6.7	5.8	5.9	7.2	6.3	6.2	5.7
Service & finance	3.2	4.3	4.0	3.8	4.6	4.1	4.1	3.9
Finance, insurance, & real estate	1.8	2.9	2.6	2.4	3.3	3.1	2.7	2.5

[a] Except food and kindred products; textile mill products; apparel and other finished textile products; and printing and publishing industry.

Source: Data on selected industries for 1957–60 are from U.S. Department of Labor, Bureau of Labor Statistics, Employment and Earnings, Annual Supplement Issue, Vol. 8, November 1961, Table SA-33, p. 100; for 1961–64, from "Special Labor Force Report, No. 52," reprint from Monthly Labor Review, April 1965, Table F–2, p. A–35.

Table 2.   Unemployment Rates: U.S. Average and by Occupation Groups Pertinent to Water Resource Projects, 1957–64 (unemployed as per cent of civilian labor force)

Occupation	1957	1958	1959	1960	1961	1962	1963	1964
U.S. average	4.3	6.8	5.5	5.6	6.7	5.6	5.7	5.2
Professional, technical, & kindred workers	1.2	2.0	1.7	1.7	2.0	1.7	1.8	1.7
Other technical & kindred workers[a]	1.3	2.4	2.0	2.1	2.5	2.0	2.2	1.9
Managers, officials, & proprietors, except farm	1.0	1.7	1.3	1.4	1.8	1.5	1.5	1.4
Clerical & kindred workers	2.8	4.4	3.7	3.8	4.6	3.9	4.0	3.7
Others[b]	3.0	4.7	3.8	4.0	4.9	4.1	4.2	3.8
Sales workers	2.6	4.0	3.7	3.7	4.7	4.1	4.2	3.4
Craftsmen, foremen, & kindred workers	3.8	6.8	5.3	5.3	6.3	5.1	4.8	4.2
Carpenters	8.1	11.7	9.4	10.1	12.3	9.4	9.6	8.4
Construction craftsmen, except carpenters	6.4	9.7	8.9	8.9	10.7	8.8	8.7	7.0
Mechanics & repairmen	2.8	5.2	3.6	3.6	4.7	3.6	3.5	3.3
Metal craftsmen, except mechanics	2.6	7.7	4.4	4.5	6.2	3.4	3.4	2.5
Other craftsmen & kindred workers	2.4	5.1	3.7	3.3	3.4	3.4	2.9	2.9
Foremen, NEC	1.7	3.0	2.3	2.1	2.6	2.6	1.9	1.7
Operatives & kindred workers	6.3	10.9	7.6	8.0	9.6	7.5	7.4	6.5
Drivers & deliverymen	4.2	6.9	5.0	5.5	6.7	5.7	5.2	4.9
Others	6.7	11.9	8.2	8.6	10.3	7.9	8.0	6.9
Service workers, except private household	5.1	7.4	6.4	6.0	7.4	6.4	6.2	6.1
Protective service workers	1.9	3.2	3.2	2.4	3.7	2.8	2.6	2.1
Laborers, except farm & mine	9.4	14.9	12.4	12.5	14.5	12.4	12.1	10.6
Construction	n.a.	21.3	19.0	19.3	21.7	20.4	20.5	16.5

NEC means not elsewhere classified; n.a. means not available.
[a] Except medical and other health workers, and teachers, except college.
[b] Except stenographers, typists, and secretaries.
Source: Data on selected occupations for 1957–60 are from U.S. Department of Labor, Bureau of Labor Statistics, *Employment and Earnings, Annual Supplement Issue,* Vol. 8, November 1961, Table SA–34, p. 101; for 1961–64, from "Special Labor Force Report, No. 52," reprint from *Monthly Labor Review,* April 1965, Table F–3, p. A–36.

consistently below 4 per cent. The other relevant occupations had a mixed pattern of unemployment over the years.

It would be useful to have occupational unemployment histories by geographic areas, but such data are not available. An alternative is use of the occupational unemployment data obtained from the Census of Population. While these data are not directly comparable to those in Table 2, they show in a general way the unemployment rates by occupational group for the United States for comparison with any selected geographic area. Table 3 illustrates this by comparing occupational unemployment rates for the census years 1950 and 1960 of West Virginia—an Appalachian state—to those of the United States as a whole.

Census data suggest that, in 1950, the occupational unemployment rates were not higher for West Virginia than for the United States as a whole. For 1960, however, West Virginia shows significantly higher unemployment rates than does the nation at large. From census data for only the two years, it is impossible to determine whether this difference represents an unstable relationship or whether the 1960 census data represent a progressively deteriorating situation in West Virginia relative to the rest of the nation. However, assuming unemployment by occupation is closely correlated with total unemployment, insured unemployment rates for both from 1949 through 1965 show a consistently higher rate of unemployment in West Virginia relative to the rest of the nation for fifteen of the seventeen years (see Table 4). These data are consistent with a presumption of significant regional differences in unemployment rates by occupation.

From our review of the employment performance of the economy during the postwar period—particularly 1957 and subsequent years—it appears that there have been long periods during which the economy has operated with considerable slack. This is apparent whether the unemployment rates are by industry, by occupation, or by region. There has been persistent unemployment, and in some cases at very high rates, particularly in these occupational skills most needed in constructing water resource projects: the carpenters, other construction craftsmen,

Table 3. Unemployment Rates by Occupation, West Virginia and the United States, 1950 and 1960 (unemployed as per cent of civilian labor force)

	1950		1960	
Occupation	W. Va.	U.S.	W. Va.	U.S.
Professional, technical, & kindred workers	0.9	1.6	1.3	1.4
Engineers, technical	1.0	1.7	1.2	1.2
Professional, technical, NEC	2.4	3.1	2.3	1.7
Managers, officials, & proprietors, except farm	0.8	1.2	1.8	1.5
Clerical & kindred workers	1.8	2.5	4.1	3.2
Sales workers	2.7	2.9	4.5	3.4
Craftsmen, foremen, & kindred workers	3.9	4.9	9.0	5.4
Carpenters	7.2	7.4	17.4	11.4
Cement & concrete finishers	14.0	9.9	27.6	14.5
Cranemen, derrickmen, & hoisters	2.1	3.7	6.4	6.1
Electricians	2.3	4.6	6.6	5.2
Excavating, grading, & machine operators	3.7	5.2	20.6	11.9
Foremen, NEC	0.8	1.2	3.9	2.0
Construction	2.7	3.1	15.2	6.1
Operatives & kindred workers	3.3	4.9	11.6	7.4
Truck & tractor drivers	4.4	4.9	10.4	6.4
Others	3.3	5.1	9.5	7.7
Service workers, except private household	3.9	5.0	6.6	5.6
Protective service workers	2.0	2.7	5.0	2.6
Laborers, except farm and mine	7.7	9.0	18.7	12.0
Construction	12.6	13.4	32.0	18.5

NEC means not elsewhere classified.
Source: U.S. Department of Commerce, Bureau of the Census, "Occupational Characteristics," *U.S. Census of Population: 1960,* Final Report PC(2)-7A (Washington, 1963).

Table 4.   Insured Unemployment Rates for West Virginia and the United States, 1949–65 (as insured unemployed per cent of average covered employment)

Year	West Virginia	United States
1949	5.9	6.0
1950	5.1	4.7
1951	3.0	3.0
1952	4.2	3.0
1953	4.3	2.8
1954	10.3	5.1
1955	5.3	3.5
1956	3.3	3.2
1957	3.8	3.6
1958	11.0	6.4
1959	8.3	4.4
1960	7.5	4.8
1961	8.4	5.6
1962	6.8	4.4
1963	5.9	4.3
1964	4.6	3.8
1965	3.6	3.0

Source: Thomas W. Gavett, *The Unemployed in West Virginia*, West Virginia University Business and Economic Studies, Vol. 8, June 1962, pp. 28–29; and U.S. Department of Labor, Manpower Administration, *Statistical Tables on Manpower: A Reprint from the 1966 Manpower Report* (Washington, 1966), Table D–4, p. 209.

and construction laborers. In the light of such persistent unemployment, distributed significantly among those crafts and skills upon which water resource projects draw, an examination of the quantitative significance for benefit-cost investment criteria seems clearly warranted. This is particularly so if such unemployment tends to be associated with the under-utilization of those types of industrial capacity upon which such project construction most heavily depends.

UTILIZATION OF POSTWAR CAPACITY IN THE U.S. ECONOMY

Since the problem of defining industrial capacity is a difficult one, the measurement of utilization is elusive.[14] However, it may only appear to be more difficult at present than the definition of full employment and its measurement,[15] or the measurement of production.[16] Several measures of

[14] For a discussion of the problems, see Almarin Phillips, "Industrial Capacity, An Appraisal of Measures of Capacity," *American Economic Review*, Papers and Proceedings of the Seventy-fifth Annual Meeting, Vol. 53 (May 1963), pp. 275–92; Lawrence Klein, *Measures of Productive Capacity*, Hearings before the Subcommittee on Economic Statistics of the Joint Economic Committee, 87 Cong. 2 sess. (1962), pp. 53 ff.; Bert G. Hickman, *Investment Demand and U.S. Economic Growth* (Washington: Brookings Institution, 1965), Chap. 5.

[15] See Seymour Harris, Introduction to Symposium, "How Much Unemployment?" *Review of Economics and Statistics*, Vol. 32 (February 1950), pp. 49–79.

[16] See Frank R. Garfield, "Measurement of Industrial Production Since 1939," *Journal of the American Statistical Association*, Vol. 39 (December 1944), pp. 439–54.

capacity and the utilization of capacity have been achieved by employing different methods. Although differences exist, both with respect to the definition of capacity and with the estimate of its utilization rate, these differences appear primarily in the magnitude of the estimated utilization rates rather than in the direction of movement from year to year.[17]

For the purpose of reviewing the relation between capacity and output in the postwar period, we use data developed by the Economic Research Unit of the Wharton School of Finance and Commerce (as described in Appendix 8). The choice of the Wharton School's capacity data is based on the relative conservatism of its estimates of excess industrial capacity, and the ready availability of such estimates for the industries which are most pertinent for the construction of water resource projects.

Figure 3 shows the relationship between output and capacity as a utilization ratio for both industrial capacity and combined industrial and service capacity for the years 1947–65. Except for the period immediately following reconversion, some excess capacity has been available continuously from 1947 to 1965. Table 5 gives a breakdown by industrial groups for the more recent period, 1957–65.

FIGURE 3. THE WHARTON SCHOOL INDEX OF RATE OF UTILIZATION OF INDUSTRIAL AND SERVICE CAPACITY IN THE UNITED STATES, 1947–65

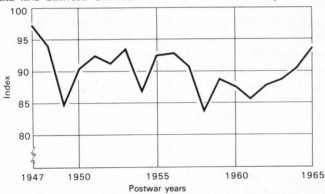

Source: Economics Research Unit, Department of Economics, Wharton School of Finance and Commerce, University of Pennsylvania. See also Appendix 8.

The work of various scholars or organizations suggests that considerable excess industrial capacity has existed in the postwar U.S. economy. As shown in Table 5, this is true at the levels of both broad aggregation of capacity and the disaggregated groups. If industrial groups in the economy have idle capacity and relevant occupational groups have substantial unemployment, output can be increased with opportunity costs that are less than the money payments for factor services. As ex-

[17] Hickman, *op. cit.,* p. 144.

Table 5.   Estimated Excess or Idle Capacity by Industry Groups Pertinent to Water Resource Projects, 1957–65 (per cent of total capacity)

Industry groups	1957	1958	1959	1960	1961	1962	1963	1964	1965
Total U.S. industrial & service	9.2	16.3	11.3	12.3	14.3	12.1	11.2	9.5	6.3
Manufacturing:									
Lumber, furniture, & allied products	16.4	17.9	8.1	14.6	16.6	13.8	12.1	10.7	8.3
Stone, clay, & glass products	13.4	22.2	12.3	17.4	22.7	22.3	20.4	17.0	15.1
Primary metals manufacturing	12.3	32.7	24.6	24.8	27.2	24.7	19.5	10.4	5.8
Fabricated metal products	5.7	14.5	4.9	8.7	15.1	12.1	11.8	10.2	4.6
Nonelectrical machinery & equipment	19.1	35.5	25.1	25.5	29.4	23.3	21.1	14.4	6.2
Electrical machinery	17.0	30.1	19.6	19.8	22.1	17.0	18.1	17.0	8.9
Transportation equipment[a]	23.4	43.8	27.3	19.6	29.4	17.7	13.1	12.6	.6
Petroleum products	2.8	6.2	2.0	1.8	3.2	3.0	3.1	3.2	4.4
Chemical & allied products	2.2	10.0	5.4	7.9	9.8	7.6	5.1	4.3	2.4
Electricity	1.1	4.1	.9	0.2	0.9	1.0	1.8	1.5	.3
Crude petroleum	3.4	11.9	9.7	12.0	12.3	12.5	11.8	12.3	13.0

[a] Including motor vehicles.

Source: Preliminary estimates from Economics Research Unit, Department of Economics, Wharton School of Finance and Commerce, University of Pennsylvania. Later estimates can be found in Lawrence R. Klein and Robert Summers, *The Wharton Index of Capacity Utilization*, Studies in Quantitative Economics No. 1, Economics Research Unit (Philadelphia: University of Pennsylvania, 1966).

pected, a comparison of the industrial representation in Tables 1 and 5 reveals a considerable correspondence between labor unemployment by industry group and excess or idle capacity by industry. In those tables, for comparable industry groups, only the production of nonelectrical machinery and chemicals does not show the pattern of coincidence.[18] Accordingly, there is reason to believe that neither insufficient skilled labor nor inadequate capacity constrained the level of output, and hence, the employment of additional factors. Moreover, it appears that there has been a considerable period during which these observations persisted. While conditions of employment were improved by the time of this writing (1967), we expect that there will again be periods during which the economy, although growing, will not be growing at a sufficient rate to absorb all new entrants into the labor force.

SUMMARY AND CONCLUSIONS

The postwar experience suggests the need for a systematic evaluation of the relevance of unemployment and excess capacity to criteria for public expenditures. Such an undertaking involves two quite different problems. On the one hand, it is necessary to consider the opportunity cost of factor services employed in the construction of public projects. This cost depends on the employment conditions experienced by relevant industries, occupations, and regions during the period of project construction. On the other hand, it is necessary to estimate the net

[18] Unemployment in these industries appears to have been significantly lower, and thus represents less slack in the industry than one would be led to expect when referring to the unutilized capacity as an index.

gains in income and employment associated with the *operation of the facilities following their construction* in areas of chronic labor surplus.

The nature of both problems is recognized in this study but only the former is explicitly treated. We restrict the scope of our effort to estimating the opportunity cost of public works built in periods of less than full employment, using investments in the water resource sector as an example. While the analytic framework is applied only to investments in the development of water resources, it has general applicability to expenditures in all areas of the public sector. The models developed in Chapters II, III, and IV will process any bill of goods associated with any new public (or private) investment. And while beyond the scope of this study, we hope that the models will be used to obtain comparative data on all alternatives for public expenditure by appropriate federal agencies.

THE SECTORAL IMPACT OF PUBLIC
INVESTMENT: A NATIONAL ANALYSIS

II

AN EVALUATION of the social cost of a public expenditure requires two steps. First is the disaggregation of the demands which the expenditure imposes on the economy into as fine detail as the data warrant. Next is a comparison of these demands with the existing pattern of unemployment. Here and in the next chapter, the first step of this procedure is taken. Empirical analyses based on input-output models are used to sort out the demands which public expenditures for water resources developments impose on the economy. Chapter IV deals with the second step in the evaluation of social costs. In these three chapters, the projects analyzed are a sample of those constructed by the U.S. Army Corps of Engineers and the Bureau of Reclamation of the U.S. Department of the Interior.

This chapter starts with a description of the empirical model of sectoral impact which we shall statistically implement. Here, the assumptions of the model are stated and its rationale defended. In the second section, we specify the nature of the data inputs necessary to implement the model and their sources. Finally, we present the empirical results of the analysis and establish a set of generalizations based on the evidence presented.

THE NATIONAL SECTORAL DEMAND MODEL

The problem of tracing the impact of a public investment expenditure on the resources of an economy is conceptually identical to that of tracing the resource impact of any other final expenditure. In each case, the task is to follow each dollar of an original expenditure as it passes through the several layers of transactions, until it culminates as a payment for the use of some primary factor of production. Consequently, this is a general model applicable to all expenditures, whether public or private.

Although our model, based on the Leontief linear input-output system,[1] permits an evaluation of the sectoral impact of a final expenditure

---

[1] For a detailed discussion of the characteristics and assumptions of the Leontief model, see Wassily W. Leontief, *The Structure of the American Economy, 1919–1939* (2nd ed. enlarged; New York: Oxford University Press, 1951); and Wassily Leontief *et al.*, *Studies in the Structure of the American Economy* (New York: Oxford University Press, 1953). In this model the primary impact of a final

15

on the economy, it does not provide a description of the entire impact. For example, it does not estimate the size or sectoral impact of the benefit stream generated by the operation of the completed project for which the expenditure is made. Also, while the model permits us to trace an expenditure throughout the economy until it is transformed into income to a primary factor of production, the impact of any additional spending which might be generated by the income receipts is not estimated in the model. This re-spending, or multiplier, effect indicates an entirely new circuit of sectoral impacts which the model could handle if it were known which commodities the recipients of final income would purchase with the additional increments to their income. Finally, the model does not evaluate the further sectoral impact on the economy arising from additional investment expenditures which might be generated by the original expenditure. Again, the model could evaluate the sectoral impact of these further final expenditures, if we knew their volume and composition.[2] Consequently, while the model does estimate the primary sectoral impact of a final expenditure, it does not permit a description of all the repercussion effects.

This general model is designed first to permit the analyst to decompose any dollar of expenditure for a final good into its detailed sectoral

---

expenditure is that which arises from the direct production sequence set into motion by the expenditure. The model is constrained by four assumptions: (1) All producers increase their output by an amount equal to the additional demand which the autonomous final demand levies on them (no inventory depletion). (2) All producers increase their demands on other producers and factor suppliers by an amount that is just sufficient to meet their output demands—which are defined by a set of technical coefficients describing the marginal relationships between inputs and outputs for each sector. (3) The demands which producers levy on other producers are for current inputs only and are not for either increases in capacity or the replacement of plant and equipment worn out in the process of production. (4) There are no lags in the sequence of generated demands and output responses. While the marginal relationships determine the impact of an expenditure on the economy, the coefficients employed are average input-output coefficients. Although the actual marginal and average relationships may be equal, there is no reason why they need be equal.

[2] The impacts generated by these additional consumption and investment expenditures could be evaluated by the application of conventional multiplier and accelerator principles. To pursue the sectoral impact of the additional consumption expenditures would require individual commodity consumption functions for each of the spending units with dissimilar spending patterns. See Hendrik Houthakker and Lester D. Taylor, *Consumer Demand in the United States, 1929–1970* (Cambridge: Harvard University Press, 1966). Similarly, to pursue the sectoral impact of generated investment expenditures would require a dynamic model incorporating individual capital investment functions for each industrial sector. Work to construct a model incorporating these effects is currently under way at the Inter-Agency Economic Growth Study Project. See Jack Alterman, "Studies of Long-Term Economic Growth," *Monthly Labor Review*, August 1965, pp. 983–87, and U.S. Department of Labor, Bureau of Labor Statistics, *Projections 1970—Interindustry Relationships, Potential Demand, Employment* (Washington, 1966).

components, and then to allocate these components to the various original contributors of the output in proportion to the value of their contribution. The categories of final contribution to which each dollar of final expenditure is allocated are:

1) The employee compensation generated by the expenditure, by occupational category.
2) The net interest payments generated by the expenditure, by industry.
3) The capital consumption allowances (depreciation) called forth by the expenditure, by industry.
4) The corporate profits generated by the expenditure, by industry.
5) The indirect business taxes required by governmental units because of the expenditure, by industry.
6) The proprietor and rental income generated by the expenditure, by industry.

Through this procedure, the contributions of labor, capital, land, and government to the final product are isolated by the occupational or industrial sector of origin within each payment category.

In the model, construction of a project is assumed to impose two primary kinds of demands on the economy: for on-site labor which represents direct factor demands, and for materials, equipment, and supplies which result in withdrawal of factors only through the several rounds of the production sequence generated by the final demand.

The detailed national sectoral demand model is described in Appendix 1. In brief, the sequential pattern of sectoral analysis pursued in the formal model is as follows: Having secured as basic data the detailed final-demand and on-site labor vectors (equation 1), we trace the gross industrial requirements generated by the final material demand through the economy by accounting for the interindustry demands imposed by industries on each other. This input-output computation, performed in equation 2, estimates the gross output required from each of eighty-two industries to produce the final demand. Equations 3 and 4 translate these gross industrial outputs into gross industrial man-year labor demands and then decompose these industrial labor requirements into 156 occupational categories. In equations 5, 7, and 8, the off-site labor costs associated with the occupational demands secured in equation 4 are estimated, adjusted, and then added to the on-site occupational labor costs to yield the occupational breakdown of total labor costs. The remaining value-added components of the bill of final goods by industry are estimated in equation 6 by applying the appropriate sets of ratios of value-added components to gross output to the data on gross output obtained in equation 2. Through this sequence, total project cost is allocated among the value-added components and then each of these components is disaggregated into either occupational or industrial detail.

PRIMARY DATA INPUTS AND THEIR SOURCES

To implement the sectoral model statistically, we need a large number of data compilations. These requirements are of two basic types: data inputs peculiar to the final expenditure which the model is to analyze and data inputs intrinsic to the model itself. In the first set of data are both the detailed final demands for material, equipment, and supply inputs (vector f) and the on-site employee compensation payments by occupation (vector i_2). In the second set are the input-output coefficients describing the interrelationship among industries in the economy (matrix A), the coefficients describing the composition of occupational requirements within each industry (matrix B), and the coefficients relating the value-added components to gross output for each industry (matrix C). Before discussing these data inputs, we shall describe the expenditure categories analyzed in the study and some basic information associated with each.

Our analysis covers forty-seven projects (listed with their locations in Appendix 2) grouped under the twelve types of water resources development construction which were named in Chapter I. For each of the twelve types, Table 6 presents the total cost, with a breakdown of the costs for: (1) material, equipment, and supplies; (2) on-site labor; and (3) other unallocated requirements. Of the total cost of $326 million for all forty-seven projects, $250 million—or roughly 75 per cent of the total—is required for a single large multiple-purpose project budgeted by the Bureau of Reclamation of the U.S. Department of the Interior. In terms of the number of projects, the largest single source of basic data was the Division of Productivity and Technological Developments of the Bureau of Labor Statistics (BLS).[3] The data which the BLS collected and analyzed related to forty-three projects chosen by stratified sampling techniques from a total of 235 contracts of the Army Corps of Engineers on which work was completed in 1960. Basic data on the remaining three projects, with a total contract cost of some $33 million, were compiled directly from detailed engineering cost estimates prepared by the Corps of Engineers. These additional projects were chosen so as to enable coverage of important categories of construction expenditure not represented by either the BLS study or the Bureau of Reclamation project.[4]

---

[3] See U.S. Department of Labor, Bureau of Labor Statistics, *Labor and Material Requirements for Civil Works Construction by the Corps of Engineers,* Bulletin No. 1390 (Washington, 1964). (Referred to hereinafter as BLS, Bulletin No. 1390.)

[4] The BLS data on material, equipment, and supply costs, as well as similar data compiled from material made available by the Corps of Engineers, are based on contract estimates prepared in the district offices of the Corps. These estimates are prepared in substantial detail for each subfeature of the project by engineers in the Corps' district offices who are familiar with local construction conditions and practices. The Bureau of Reclamation data are based on actual expenditures for project construction. For the estimates of on-site labor cost, the BLS and Reclamation

From the evidence in Table 6, it is clear that the types of project vary substantially with respect to the relative demands for on-site labor and material, equipment, and supply inputs. While over 80 per cent of the contract cost is allocated to material inputs in the case of powerhouse construction, only about 41 per cent is so allocated in the construction of levees. Taking another example, the large multiple-purpose project which we examined required 42 per cent of the total cost for on-site labor, while the construction of revetments required under 13 per cent. This variance in the structure of inputs is reflected in the ratios of material, equipment, and supply costs to on-site labor costs. While most of the ratios lie between 1.2 to 2.0, the construction of revetments bears a ratio of 5.8—over five times the 1.1 ratio for levee construction. For all projects lumped together, 53 per cent of total contract cost is allocated to materials, equipment, and supplies, while 39 per cent is allocated to on-site labor.

All other costs of the projects have been put in a residual category. The unallocated costs shown in Table 6 include contractors' tax payments, earnings from payments for rents and interest, corporate profits after taxes, and overhead (including mobilization and demobilization costs).[5] These costs as a proportion of total contract cost range from 1 per cent in the case of powerhouse construction to about 23 per cent for the construction of levees.[6]

---

data were derived from the actual construction payrolls filed by the contractors with the construction agency (as required by the Davis-Bacon Act). On-site labor costs for the remainder of the projects were compiled from detailed engineering cost estimates prepared in the Corps' district offices. See BLS, Bulletin No. 1390, *op. cit.*, for a further discussion of the estimating methodology, data sources, and techniques of adjustment.

[5] The BLS data have been adjusted in two ways and, hence, are not identical with that published in Bulletin No. 1390, *op. cit.* Both of these adjustments consist of the allocation of some of the BLS "other costs" either to costs for material, equipment, and supplies or to costs for on-site labor. First, from supplementary information it was learned that inspectors and engineers employed by the contractors are often considered as part of their overhead and, hence, are not reported as labor employed on the payroll report submitted by the contractor. On the basis of the data on the large multiple-purpose project (in which such labor costs were included in the payroll reports), estimates of costs for contractor-employed inspectors and engineers were included, where relevant, in the on-site labor cost. The transfer of these costs reduced the total unallocated cost category by an equivalent amount. The second adjustment consists of removing an additional amount of costs from the unallocated cost category and assigning it to materials, equipment, and supplies. These shifted costs consisted of such items as real estate and rental charges, finance and insurance costs, and business travel and entertainment costs which the BLS treated as overhead costs. The data utilized for this adjustment are estimates of the breakdown of material, equipment, and supply costs for all conservation and resource development. See Norman Frumkin, "Construction Activity in the 1958 Input-Output Study," *Survey of Current Business*, May 1965, pp. 13–24.

[6] The large variation in the unallocated cost category is not surprising. Some of this arises because of the difference in sources of data. For some of the sources,

Footnote continued on page 22.

Table 6. Total Construction Costs of Twelve Types of Water Resource Projects: Allocated to Industrial and Occupational Categories (in dollars per $1,000 of total contract cost)

Categories	Large earth fill dams	Small earth fill dams	Local flood protec- tion	Pile dikes
Industry & input-output study sectors				
Agriculture, forestry, & fisheries, 1–4	*	1	*	—
Mining, including crude petroleum, 5–10	*	24	41	122
Nondurable goods manufacturing, 14–19, 24–34	98	112	35	47
Durable goods manufacturing, 12–13, 20–23, 35–64	278	293	278	189
Lumber & wood products, 20–23	8	6	12	55
Stone, clay, & glass products, 35–36	14	10	69	—
Primary metals, 37–38	2	4	5	4
Fabricated metals, 39–42	56	31	126	16
Nonelectrical machinery, except construction, 43–44, 46–52	15	14	3	7
Construction machinery, 45	104	151	41	60
Electrical machinery, 53–58	2	2	1	—
Transportation equipment, 13, 59–61	77	75	21	47
Miscellaneous, 12, 62–64	*	*	*	—
Transportation & warehousing, 65	16	31	38	88
Wholesale & retail trade, 69	115	116	82	69
Services, 66–68, 70–82	27	27	27	27
Total material, equipment, & supply cost[a]	533	603	502	543
Occupation				
Professional, technical, managerial, clerical, & kindred workers	37	26	29	42
Craftsmen, foremen, & kindred workers	157	202	214	137
Carpenters	18	9	45	5
Cement finishers	3	1	10	—
Iron & metal workers	3	1	29	—
Construction equipment operators	51	134	80	80
Other building trades	2	1	1	—
Mechanics	18	20	9	1
Labor foremen	21	26	30	11
Others	41	10	10	40
Operatives & kindred workers	79	51	63	84
Truck & tractor drivers	49	9	36	32
Sailors & deck hands	—	—	—	21
Others	30	42	27	31
Service workers	—	—	—	—
Laborers	40	40	72	35
Total on-site labor cost[a]	312	320	379	298
Total unallocated cost	155	77	119	159
Total project cost[a]	1,000	1,000	1,000	1,000
Total contract cost (in $ thousand)[b]	11,138	5,440	6,645	1,544
Number of projects of each type	1	3	3	5
Ratio of total material, equipment, & supply cost to total on-site labor costs	1.71	1.88	1.32	1.82

Asterisk (*) means less than $.50, but greater than zero; dash (—) means zero.

[a] Columns may not add because of rounding.

[b] Refers to the total cost in each category from which the detailed breakdowns in dollars per $1,000 of total contract cost were computed.

Source: The names and locations of the projects which were analyzed are given in Appendix 2. The

Levees	Revetments	Powerhouse construction	Medium concrete dams	Lock & concrete dams	Large multiple-purpose projects	Dredging	Miscellaneous	Total
*	—	*	*	1	—	—	1	
73	303	8	2	66	41	*	23	
90	45	7	20	20	26	103	121	
109	99	659	369	450	319	250	282	
1	46	12	5	5	6	*	20	
1	*	14	94	120	60	—	54	
1	4	13	33	67	35	45	36	
10	9	41	83	52	77	21	5	
1	*	255	46	57	43	1	10	
72	20	24	84	109	44	32	107	
*	—	293	3	19	46	*	*	
23	20	4	21	21	6	151	50	
*	—	3	*	—	2	*	*	
54	193	22	19	61	39	17	35	
56	73	90	84	99	61	56	106	
27	27	26	41	26	27	28	27	
409	740	810	533	723	514	453	597	
51	13	25	55	27	63	132	37	
170	37	108	176	155	253	56	132	
1	*	26	30	28	47	—	14	
—	—	2	4	4	4	—	2	
*	*	13	17	6	22	—	—	
90	21	8	33	47	43	4	56	
—	—	32	23	23	35	1	*	
27	*	*	3	11	5	4	15	
12	6	14	25	24	45	7	5	
40	10	13	41	12	52	40	40	
105	35	27	60	47	28	131	78	
54	4	3	14	24	8	1	41	
18	21	—	—	1	—	68	—	
33	10	24	46	22	20	62	37	
—	—	—	—	—	—	8	—	
36	44	18	68	32	72	39	32	
362	127	178	358	260	416	365	278	
229	133	11	109	17	70	182	125	
1,000	1,000	1,000	1,000	1,000	1,000	1,000	1,000	
2,370	1,756	7,793	16,518	9,020	249,741	10,092	4,177	326,234
7	5	1	1	1	1	15	4	47
1.13	5.83	4.54	1.49	2.78	1.24	1.24	2.15	

industrial categories and input-output sector numbers are based on the list of 82 industries in Appendix 7. The occupational categories are adapted from the list of 156 occupations given in Appendix 3. Because of differences in statistical sources and methods of consolidation, the industrial and occupational categories here are not in most cases directly comparable to those in Tables 1, 3, and 5.

Primary Expenditure Data

As a first step in implementing the sectoral model for each type of project, the components of the material, equipment, and supply costs are isolated by detailed industry and the components of the on-site labor costs are disaggregated into detailed occupations. These breakdowns, aggregated to larger industrial and occupational groupings, are the ones shown in the body of Table 6. To secure the breakdown of material, equipment, and supply costs—that is, the bills of final demand—a breakdown of the dollar cost of all the material, equipment, and supply inputs to project construction was obtained in 4-digit Standard Industrial Classification detail. This array of expenditures for each type of project was then aggregated into the industries appropriate to the 1958 input-output study of the Office of Business Economics of the U.S. Department of Commerce.[7] It is this 82-sector breakdown which is represented by vector *x* in the formal model shown in Appendix 1.

To place these data in the form shown in Table 6, a number of adjustments were made in the basic data we collected. First, the data on material inputs obtained from all of the sources were expressed in terms of "purchaser value"—the number of units purchased times the amount per delivered unit paid by the purchaser. Both transportation and warehouse charges and wholesale and retail trade margins are included. To isolate these components for each unit of input, a set of transportation and trade factors was applied to all dollar demands, by 4-digit Standard Industrial Classification category.[8] Through this technique, the transportation and trade components were eliminated from the purchaser value, leaving the material requirement stated in terms of "producer value"—

---

for example, the profit margin was built into the estimates, which accounts for a relatively stable addition to total contract costs. In other cases, where the estimates are based on actual costs, profit margins may be very high or very low (or negative), depending on the circumstances of the individual project. This, for example, accounts for the very low amount of unallocated costs for the large multiple-purpose project. Because of the erratic nature of construction profit margins, this kind of variation would occur among projects of the same type as well as different types. Another source of variation stems from differences in the structure of inputs into project construction. In a case in which a substantial share of the total cost is composed of the purchase of large pieces of equipment (for example, turbines and generators), one would expect the contractor's profits to be a relatively small share of the total project cost. This, for example, accounts for the small figure under unallocated costs associated with powerhouse construction. See BLS, Bulletin No. 1390, *op. cit.*, pp. 12–13, for a further discussion of factors accounting for variation among project types and among individual projects.

[7] Morris R. Goldman, Martin L. Marimont, and Beatrice N. Vaccara, "The Interindustry Structure of the United States: A Report on the 1958 Input-Output Study," *Survey of Current Business*, November 1964, pp. 10–29.

[8] The trade and transportation factors applied in this transformation were prepared by the Office of Business Economics in connection with the 1958 input-output study.

the number of units purchased valued at the producers' prices.[9] Through this transformation, the purchaser can be thought of as buying *n* units of the good at the producer price plus a certain quantity of transportation, distribution, and marketing services.

A second adjustment was made to convert all of the input costs of materials from their stated values to values of a given base year, 1958.[10] Even though nearly all of the project inputs analyzed were stated in prices of the years 1957 to 1962—a period when price levels were nearly stable—it was essential that they be placed on a common basis because of the substantial (though offsetting) movement of individual commodity prices. This conversion involved the application of an appropriate series of product price deflators to the input data arranged in the 4-digit Standard Industrial Classification categories.[11]

Finally, for each of the bills of final demand, the "rental cost" of heavy construction equipment—defined as the cost of owning (depreciation) and maintaining equipment—was assigned to the relevant equipment manufacturing industry.[12] Two things should be noted about this procedure. First, these estimates of depreciation may not be the same as the actual depreciation estimates made by the specific contractors in the projects studied. Rather, they are based on assumptions as to the quantity, age, type, and value of the units of plant available and required for project construction.[13] Second, the procedure of assigning these estimates to the relevant production sectors is equivalent to assuming that the owners of equipment keep constant the value of construction equipment inventory. For every dollar of equipment "worn out," it is assumed that a dollar is spent to purchase new equipment.[14]

In comparing the bills of final demand of the different types of project, three primary characteristics stand out. First is the enormous variability in the pattern of industrial demands among the project types. Even though all are civil works installations in the water resources area, there

[9] This adjustment was required by the producer-value basis of the 1958 input-output coefficients used to trace the interindustry requirements of these final material, equipment, and supply demands.

[10] The year 1958 was chosen as the base period in order to place both the value of final demands and the input-output coefficients on the same value basis.

[11] The product price deflators were prepared by the Office of Business Economics from basic data obtained by the Division of Industrial Prices and Price Indexes of the Bureau of Labor Statistics.

[12] As in the case of the other material costs, estimates of depreciation by type of equipment were derived from the engineering contract cost estimates developed by the Corps of Engineers as described earlier.

[13] For a more detailed discussion of the treatment of equipment depreciation, see BLS, Bulletin No. 1390, pp. 27–28.

[14] This assumption may be close to reality for those large-scale projects in which pieces of construction equipment are both purchased for use on the project and "used up" as the project is constructed. This procedure is equivalent to treating equipment purchases as current inputs. Because they are technically capital purchases, the earlier assumption that purchases are on current account only becomes somewhat modified in the treatment of the construction industry.

is only the vaguest sort of uniformity in the make-up of material demands among projects. For example, while the construction of revetments makes large demands on the mining industry for stone and gravel inputs, the construction of lock and concrete dams allocates the bulk of its demands to durable goods sectors—in particular, to machinery and equipment manufactures and to stone, clay, and glass products.

Despite this lack of general conformity, however, a second characteristic is the fact that a number of individual industries or industry groups experience heavy final-output demands from nearly all of the project types. Industries providing transportation equipment and construction machinery are important suppliers of inputs to nearly all types of projects. For each type at least $20 per $1,000 of total contract cost is spent on construction machinery; in all except two types, at least $20 per $1,000 is spent on transportation equipment. With somewhat less regularity, the mining industry fills a significant portion of the output demands; for example, in eight of the twelve project types, mining supplies more than $20 per $1,000 of total contract cost.

A final characteristic of the bills of final demand is the heavy requirements which all impose on the transportation and trade sectors. In no case is the demand on the trade sector less than $56 per $1,000 of contract cost, and in three of the twelve types it exceeds $100. In nine of the twelve, the demand for transportation services exceeds $20 per $1,000 of contract cost, and in four it is over $50. For one case, revetments, the transportation services account for nearly 20 per cent of the total contract cost.

The middle section of Table 6 displays the occupational breakdown of the on-site labor cost for each type of project. The labor cost represented here refers to payments made to those workers actually engaged on the site in the physical construction of the project. As noted above, these data were obtained from payroll reports filed by contractors for most of the projects analyzed. In the case of projects for which the data were compiled directly from engineering cost estimates of the Corps, the on-site labor information was taken directly from the latest contract cost estimates made before construction started.[15]

Almost all project types impose heavy demands on the operators of construction equipment (including workers who operate trucks and tractors). In seven of the twelve cases, over 25 per cent of the total on-site labor cost was allocated to these occupations. In all of the project types except dredging and revetments, over 45 per cent of the total on-site labor demands appears in the major occupation group which includes the construction equipment operators—that is, in the category of crafts-

[15] Overtime hours have a considerable effect on the total on-site wage costs of these projects. It is estimated that between 15 and 25 per cent of the man-hours worked on these projects are overtime hours. See BLS, Bulletin No. 1390, *op. cit.*, pp. 14–18.

men, foremen, and kindred workers. As in the case of industrial demands, there is variation among project types also in the patterns of final demand for on-site labor. For example, projects for levee construction, medium concrete dams, and dredging impose markedly different patterns of on-site demands on the labor market.[16] Finally, the relatively small demands imposed by project construction on unskilled labor should be noted. Only for the construction of revetments does the cost of unskilled labor exceed 20 per cent of the total on-site labor cost. More significantly, in no case does the demand for on-site unskilled labor absorb as much as 8 per cent of total contract cost. This low demand is of major importance in considering water resource projects as potential sources of appropriate labor demand for depressed, impacted, or high unemployment regions such as Appalachia.

Data Intrinsic to the Model

In addition to the data inputs peculiar to the expenditures to be analyzed, implementation of the model requires three basic data inputs intrinsic to the model itself. As noted earlier, the first of these are the technical coefficients defining the interindustry relationships in the economy, and these are represented by matrix A in the formal model. In this study, we use the 1958 national input-output coefficients prepared by the Office of Business Economics.[17] These estimates, which were prepared as an integral part of the national income accounts, are expressed in an 82-order matrix of input-output coefficients for the year 1958 in producer value. From the data generated by the input-output study, the following information can be obtained for any bill of final demand: (1) the structure of intermediate goods purchased from any industry by each of the other industries, (2) the structure of gross outputs required from each industry in order to yield the final demand, and (3) the value added by any industry in producing its gross output.

The second group of data intrinsic to the model is made up of the ratios of each of the components of value added to gross output for each industry. These components are defined precisely as employee compensation, net interest, capital consumption charges (depreciation), indirect business taxes, corporate profits, and proprietor and rental income. With these ratios, represented by matrix C in the formal model, it is possible to isolate the components of the value added by any industry caused by the imposition of the final demand. To calculate these ratios, 1958 data

[16] Because each of these three project types have a total on-site labor cost figure in the neighborhood of $360, the variation among project categories in the relative importance of different occupations can be seen by a direct comparison of the dollar per $1,000 of contract cost values.
[17] See Goldman, Marimont, and Vaccara, *op. cit.*; Frumkin, *op. cit.*, and National Economics Division Staff, "The Transactions Table of the 1958 Input-Output Study and Revised Direct and Total Requirements Data," *Survey of Current Business*, September 1965, pp. 33–49.

on the value of the total of each component for each industry were obtained and placed as numerator over the gross output of each industry.[18] For each industry, the sum of these components for 1958 equals 1958 value added. For the nation, their sum equals gross national product—that is, the national bill of final demand.

Maintaining the assumption of linearity made earlier, the combination of the bills of final demand, the input-output matrix, and these ratios of value-added components permits the gross output required by any bill of final demand to be calculated for each industry and decomposed into the value-added components (wages, profits, interest, etc.), also by industry. In the formal model presented in Appendix 1, this calculation is summarized in equations 2 and 6. By definition, the value-added figures summed across industries equal the value of the bill of final demand. This definition is stated in equations 9 and 10 of the model.

The final input of data intrinsic to the model is the matrix of occupational labor coefficients for each industry necessary to estimate the occupational breakdown of the off-site labor requirements generated by the bills of final demand. As described in equations 3 and 4 of the model, the gross output requirements of each industry are first transformed into man-years of labor demand, and then these aggregate man-year figures are decomposed into their occupational components and summed across industries. In this transformation, 1958 dollar values of gross output become 1960 man-year labor requirements by the application of a set of factors expressing 1960 industrial employment in man-years per 1958 dollar of industrial output.[19] By multiplying these industrial man-year

[18] The ratios of total value added to gross output, by industry, were obtained directly from the 1958 study. See Goldman, Marimont, and Vaccara, *op. cit.* The 1958 industry data on the value-added components were obtained from two sources. The industry data on employee compensation, capital consumption charges, and corporate profits were obtained directly from the Office of Business Economics. Similar data on the remaining components of value added are from the substantially less detailed material in Martin L. Marimont, "GNP by Major Industries," *Survey of Current Business*, October 1962, pp. 6–18. Included under proprietor and rental income are the surpluses less subsidies of government enterprises. Indirect business taxes include business transfer payments. Corporate profits include adjustments for inventory valuation. In the data obtained from both sources, the number of detailed industries is less than the number of industries in the input-output matrix. The industries with detailed data number, respectively, 55 and 15. For those input-output industries which were subindustries of the more grossly defined industries in the value-added component data, the ratios of the 1958 value-added component (for example, employee compensation) to 1958 value added for the entire industry were assigned to each of the subindustries. In those cases in which, because of the differences in industry detail, the value-added components failed to add to the total industry value added published in the 1958 input-output study, either proprietor and rental income or indirect business tax was estimated as residuals.

[19] The change from 1958 values to 1960 values is required to permit use of the occupation-by-industry matrix. The employment-output factors referred to were prepared by the Division of Productivity and Technological Developments of the Bureau of Labor Statistics for use with the 1958 input-output study.

labor requirements by the appropriate occupational coefficients, the occupational breakdown of total off-site labor costs for each type of project is obtained.

The matrix of occupational coefficients by industry employed in this computation (matrix C) was constructed from 1960 data of the Division of Occupational Employment Statistics of the Bureau of Labor Statistics. This matrix contains occupational coefficients for 137 industries and 156 occupations.[20] In performing the calculation which yielded the occupational breakdown of off-site man-year labor requirements for each project type,[21] the linearity assumption made earlier is maintained—that is, as an industry expands, its occupational structure is assumed to remain constant.

To transform the man-year labor requirements into occupational labor costs, an estimate of the average annual wage and salary income earned by individuals in each occupational category was multiplied by the man-year requirements. These average annual wage and salary estimates were calculated from the 1960 Census of Population. The population group used to form these estimates was made up of members of the experienced civilian labor force who worked fifty to fifty-two weeks in 1959.[22]

---

[20] The ratios in the matrix were latter stage although preliminary estimates and have not yet been published. For a more detailed description of the matrix see U.S. Department of Labor, Bureau of Labor Statistics, *Handbook of Methods for Surveys and Studies*, Bulletin No. 1458 (Washington, 1966), Chap. 7. The primary sources used by the BLS in preparing the estimates were the 1960 Census of Population and data collected by the Bureau of the Census through the Current Population Survey. For a detailed description of sources, see U.S. Department of Labor, Bureau of Labor Statistics, *Occupational Employment Statistics, Sources, and Data*, Report No. 305 (Washington, June 1966). The titles of the 156 occupations included in the matrix are listed in Appendix 3.

[21] As already noted, while the gross output figures emerging from the input-output computation are in 82-industry detail, the occupation-industry matrix contains 137 industrial sectors. Two possibilities existed to secure conformability: the occupation-industry matrix could be aggregated to 82 sectors or the gross output data could be expanded to 137 sectors. The latter course was chosen. Expansion of the 82 sectors into 137 was done in two steps. First, the components of the final demand or direct components of gross output (about 45 per cent of the gross output) were assigned to the appropriate industry among the 137 on the basis of the 4-digit Standard Industrial Classification category. Second, the indirect component of the gross output of these input-output industries which coincide with more than one industry in the occupation-industry matrix was distributed among the relevant industries in proportion to the distribution of national employment among these industries. Through this process, the 82-sector gross output vectors were disaggregated to the 137 occupation-industry matrix production sectors. The symbol N in the formal model signifies either the 82-sector breakdown or the 137-sector breakdown, depending on the stage of the analysis.

[22] See U.S. Department of Commerce, U.S. Bureau of the Census, "Occupational Characteristics," *U.S. Census of Population: 1960*, Final Report PC(2)–7A (Washington, 1963).

ESTIMATES OF NATIONAL SECTORAL IMPACT

The application of the final demand requirements to the computational model yields detailed sectoral demands of the expenditures considered and the decomposition of their value-added components. In summarizing these results (shown in Tables 7, 8, and 9), we compare each of the project types with respect to the magnitude of the value-added components generated by each and the industrial and occupational impacts on the economy of $1,000 of contract expenditure on each. In addition, the industrial composition of the value-added components is presented for the large multiple-purpose project.

In the body of Table 7, the gross output required from each of the aggregated industries and the occupational breakdown of labor cost required to produce the bills of final demand are presented. The breakdowns of both the gross output and the total labor cost are stated in dollar values based on the actual bills of goods.[23] From the data in this table, the industrial gross output and occupational labor requirements of the various project types can be compared with each other and the structure of industrial and occupational demands made by water resource projects can be contrasted with the existing national pattern of production and employment.

At the bottom of Table 7, the gross breakdown of the value-added components, by type of project, is shown. Also included is the 1958 breakdown of the aggregate value-added components for the entire national economy. By comparing the project types with each other and with the national summary, the impact of the alternative final expenditures on the various income-receiving sectors can be observed.

For all of the project types, labor is by far the most important single cost item. In no case do these costs fall below $500 per $1,000, or 50 per cent, of total contract cost. While total labor costs for most of the projects are between $600 and $700, there is one—the large multiple-purpose project—in which labor costs absorb nearly 72 per cent of total contract costs.

These data also permit a comparison of the potency of water resource project construction in generating labor income relative to a $1,000 expenditure for the bundle of final goods composing gross national product. Whereas the expenditure for GNP goods generates $576 worth of labor income, in all of the project types except three the comparable figure is over $600.[24]

---

[23] Appendix Table 10A–1 shows the gross output required if the total final demand in each project type is blown up to $1,000 but its structural composition kept unchanged. In Appendix Tables 10A–2 and 10A–3, the gross impact on the top ten detailed industries and occupations is shown for each project type.

[24] A part of this higher relative demand for labor is attributable to the assumptions underlying the construction of our bills of goods. Because we assumed that the stock of construction equipment remains fixed, part of what would otherwise be depreciation expense is incorporated into the bills of final goods and, hence, into further labor demands.

The cost components of value added, for other than labor costs, appear in Table 7 as relatively small items in the total contract cost. They are also substantially smaller than their counterparts nationally.[25] In only one case do they, in the aggregate, exceed 30 per cent of total contract cost or 70 per cent of their national counterparts.

Industrial Requirements

Several characteristics of the information on industrial categories are revealing. First, as with the bills of final demand, it is the Durable Goods Manufacturing industries which receive the primary impact from construction expenditures for water resource projects. In six of the cases, the *gross* demand for durable goods output exceeds $500 for every $1,000 worth of contract expenditure; in the case of powerhouse construction, the figure exceeds $1,100. Within the durable goods sector, there are individual industries which, in almost all cases, supply the major portion of the output required from that sector. In each type of project, the transportation, construction machinery, primary metals, and fabricated metals industries, taken together, furnish over 50 per cent of the supply required from the durable goods industries.

The pattern of industrial demands of those installations requiring large concrete and cement inputs is not uniform. Both the medium concrete dams and the lock and concrete dam require about 20 per cent of the total final costs for material, equipment, and supply outputs from the stone, clay, and glass products industry. However, the characteristics of individual installations substantially influence demands for cement and concrete. If the remote location of the project causes the on-site production of concrete to be cheaper than its purchase, the impact of project construction will fall more heavily in the mining[26] and nonelectrical machinery (except construction) industries.

Still within the durable goods category, the construction of a power facility has a substantial effect on the electrical machinery industry.

[25] There are three primary reasons for this. First, while we have captured and allocated substantially all of the labor costs, there remains a rather large body of costs which were residually obtained and which are included in the unallocated costs row of the table. These costs, if allocated, would be added to the nonlabor cost components of value added. Second, by the procedure adopted in constructing our bills of final demand, we have excluded the depreciation component of value added in the construction industry. By allocating this depreciation to the bills of final demand, its value becomes distributed among all of the value-added components, including labor cost. Third, the nonlabor cost components of the projects are relatively smaller than their national counterparts because of the peculiar characteristics of the industries from which the projects draw (or fail to draw) most heavily. The largest source of indirect business taxes, for example, is the tobacco industry. Public works project construction makes extremely small demands on this industry and, therefore, generates but little indirect business taxes. Likewise, the agricultural sectors have very high ratios of proprietor and rental income to gross output and of capital consumption to gross output. Again, project construction generates very little output in these sectors.

[26] More particularly, the stone and clay mining and quarrying industry.

Table 7. Twelve Project Types: Gross Output Required to Yield Final Demands by Industry, Total Labor Cost by Occupation, and Breakdown of Total Project Cost into Value-Added Components (in dollars per $1,000 of total contract cost and per cent of totals)

Categories	1958 U.S. $	%	Large earth fill dams $	%	Small earth fill dams $	%	Local flood protection $	%
Industry	*Gross output*							
Agriculture, forestry, & fisheries	6		10	1	11	1	10	1
Mining, including crude petroleum	2		61	5	81	6	81	8
Construction[a]	6		9	1	11	1	10	1
Nondurable goods manufacturing[b]	20		187	16	218	17	112	11
Durable goods manufacturing	21		514	45	549	43	480	47
Lumber & wood products	2		15	1	12	1	21	2
Stone, clay, & glass products	1		24	2	21	2	87	8
Primary metals	3		90	8	96	6	93	9
Fabricated metals	2		85	7	61	5	150	15
Nonelectrical machinery, except construction	2		48	4	55	4	26	2
Construction machinery	*		112	10	163	13	47	5
Electrical machinery	2		16	1	16	1	12	1
Transportation equipment	5		120	11	120	9	40	4
Miscellaneous	3		5	*	4	*	4	*
Transportation & warehousing	4		48	4	68	5	71	7
Wholesale & retail trade	11		146	13	152	12	112	11
Services	29		166	15	182	14	154	15
Total gross output required[e]	100		1,141	100	1,273	100	1,030	100
Occupation	*Labor cost*							
Professional, technical, & kindred workers	16		60	10	47	7	41	6
Managers, officials, & proprietors	13		59	10	74	11	61	9
Clerical & kindred workers	13		49	8	52	8	43	6
Sales workers	7		13	2	14	3	11	2
Craftsmen, foremen, & kindred workers	19		219	36	275	42	276	41
Carpenters	2		20	3	11	2	48	7
Cement finishers	*		3	1	1	*	10	2
Iron & metal workers	*		3	1	1	*	29	4
Construction equipment operators	1		53	9	137	21	84	13
Other building trades	3		7	1	7	1	9	1
Mechanics	4		9	2	10	2	9	1
Labor foremen	3		32	5	39	6	41	6
Others	7		92	15	69	10	46	7
Operatives & kindred workers	19		149	24	133	20	138	21
Truck & tractor drivers	3		59	10	21	3	51	8
Sailors & deck hands	*		**	*	**	*	**	*
Others	16		90	15	112	17	87	13
Service workers	6		7	1	8	1	7	1
Laborers, except farm	4		55	9	57	9	89	13
Farmers & farm workers	3		2	*	3	*	2	*
Total labor cost[e]	576	100	612	100	662	100	667	100
Other value-added cost components								
Net interest	15		8		9		7	
Capital consumption allowance	87		49		56		45	
Indirect business taxes	91		49		55		46	
Corporate profits	92		61		70		57	
Proprietor & rental income	139		41		44		35	
Net imports	—		22		25		21	
Unallocated costs[d]	—		155		77		119	
Total cost (income)[e]	1,000[f]		1,000		1,000		1,000	

One asterisk (*) means less than .5 per cent but greater than zero; two (**) mean less than $.50 but greater than zero.

[a] Refers only to maintenance and repair construction. In the 1958 input-output study, new construction is treated as a final demand.

[b] In all of the project types, the overwhelming supplier in the nondurable goods sector is petroleum and related products.

[e] Columns may not add because of rounding.

[d] Ideally, all of these costs could be allocated to one of the other value-added categories if the raw data were sufficiently detailed. We presume that the substantial majority of those unallocated items falls into the categories of corporate profits, proprietor and rental income, and indirect business taxes.

Pile dikes		Levees		Revetments		Power-house construction		Medium concrete dams		Lock & concrete dams		Large multiple-purpose projects		Dredging		Miscellaneous	
$	%	$	%	$	%	$	%	$	%	$	%	$	%	$	%	$	%
19	2	6	1	18	1	13	1	9	1	11	1	8	1	7	1	14	1
159	15	131	16	356	26	42	2	38	3	118	7	77	7	71	7	100	8
12	1	9	1	19	1	11	1	10	1	13	1	9	1	8	1	11	1
130	12	154	19	149	11	113	7	102	9	126	9	103	10	174	18	225	18
367	34	229	28	265	20	1,113	65	609	55	742	51	539	51	447	45	497	40
83	8	5	1	68	5	23	1	12	1	12	1	13	1	10	1	33	3
14	1	10	1	27	2	29	2	115	10	151	10	78	7	7	1	71	6
56	5	42	5	41	3	190	11	134	12	184	13	129	12	126	13	108	9
34	3	24	3	23	2	79	5	110	10	82	6	100	9	48	5	29	2
32	3	22	3	21	2	345	20	82	7	103	7	75	7	28	3	42	3
71	7	81	10	37	3	37	2	92	8	123	8	52	5	36	4	117	9
10	1	7	1	8	1	359	21	18	2	37	3	64	6	15	1	11	1
65	6	36	4	36	3	37	2	40	4	42	3	20	2	173	18	82	7
3	*	2	*	3	*	14	1	6	*	6	*	7	1	4	*	5	*
122	11	79	10	238	17	65	4	54	5	109	7	72	7	48	5	75	6
102	9	78	9	114	8	141	8	117	11	144	10	93	9	85	9	140	11
169	16	138	17	225	16	204	12	174	16	200	14	152	14	146	15	184	15
1,080	100	824	100	1,383	100	1,701	100	1,114	100	1,463	100	1,054	100	986	100	1,246	100
48	8	49	9	34	7	83	12	73	11	52	8	72	10	55	9	56	9
67	11	55	10	70	13	82	12	63	9	81	12	66	9	139	22	66	11
39	7	34	6	47	9	76	11	47	7	59	9	46	6	38	6	51	9
9	2	8	1	10	2	15	2	11	2	14	2	10	1	8	1	13	2
202	34	218	38	120	23	222	32	245	36	250	36	319	44	126	20	199	33
8	1	3	1	4	1	29	4	32	5	31	5	49	7	5	1	16	3
**	*	**	*	**	*	2	*	4	1	4	1	4	1	**	*	2	*
1	*	1	*	1	*	14	2	17	3	6	1	22	3	4	1	**	*
85	14	93	16	31	6	7	1	36	5	53	8	48	7	6	1	60	10
7	1	5	1	8	2	39	6	29	4	32	5	41	6	12	2	7	1
9	2	7	1	12	2	14	2	10	2	14	2	9	1	8	1	10	2
23	4	20	4	21	4	38	6	38	6	41	6	58	8	17	3	17	3
69	11	89	16	43	8	79	11	79	12	69	10	88	12	74	12	87	14
164	27	160	28	156	30	158	23	138	21	159	23	108	15	185	30	158	26
51	9	65	11	36	7	16	2	28	4	47	7	22	3	9	1	56	9
21	4	18	3	22	4	**	*	**	*	2	*	**	*	68	11	**	*
92	15	77	13	98	19	142	21	110	16	110	16	86	12	108	17	102	17
7	1	5	1	10	2	11	2	7	1	10	1	7	1	15	2	8	1
60	10	46	8	66	13	40	6	87	13	58	8	89	12	54	9	51	9
4	1	1	*	3	1	3	*	2	*	2	*	2	*	2	*	3	1
600	100	576	100	517	100	691	100	674	100	685	100	719	100	621	100	605	100
9		7		13		10		8		10		7		7		9	
51		41		73		65		48		66		46		42		58	
48		37		68		66		47		63		45		37		54	
55		45		71		97		65		83		59		50		70	
47		42		77		33		28		44		30		36		49	
31		22		47		29		19		29		21		22		28	
159		229		133		11		109		17		70		182		185	
1,000		1,000		1,000		1,000		1,000		1,000		1,000		1,000		1,000	

ᵉ Columns may not add because of (1) rounding and (2) the compounding of rounding errors in successive multiplications.

ᶠ It should be noted that the breakdown of the contract cost into its value-added components is not conceptually identical with the value-added breakdown of gross national product. Contract cost is defined to include the cost of imported goods and services. GNP is defined as net of imports. To make them comparable, imports could be subtracted from the contract cost and then a new value-added breakdown computed on this new cost figure. See also footnote (ᵈ) of this table.

Nearly $360 worth of output was required from this industry per $1,000 of powerhouse construction contract cost.

Two other sectors should be mentioned in regard to the gross output data in Table 7. First, the mining industry is notable in that its fortunes are highly dependent on the type of installation. Gross output requirements for extractive products range from $38 per $1,000 of contract cost to nearly ten times that amount. Second are the large and consistent demands imposed on both the transportation and trade industries. Only in one type of project—dredging—does the sum of the requirements levied on these two industries fall below $150 per $1,000 of contract cost.

A striking comparison in Table 7 is that between the pattern of output and employment in the economy and the pattern of output and labor demands which project construction imposes on the economy. Column one of Table 7 shows the industrial pattern of the gross output of the United States[27] and the occupational composition of total labor cost for the nation in percentage terms. These breakdowns are directly comparable with the percentages for each project type in the body of the table. While about 20 per cent of the economy's production occurs in the broad category of durable goods, 40 per cent or more of the gross output demands of nine of the twelve project types draws upon this broad industrial category. In individual industries, this pattern is even more extreme. For example, less than 1 per cent of the economy's gross output occurs in the construction machinery industry, but that industry supplies 5 per cent or more of the gross output requirements for ten of the twelve project types. In one type (small earth fill dams), 13 per cent of the gross output requirements are in the construction machinery industry. Or again, 1 per cent of the economy's gross output takes place in the stone, clay, and glass products industry, but in five types of projects the gross output requirements drawn from this industry range from 6 per cent to 10 per cent. Whereas 2 per cent of the economy's gross output is in the mining industry, up to 26 per cent of gross output requirements for water resource project construction are extractive products, with most of the projects requiring between 5 and 10 per cent of their gross outputs from this sector.

The agriculture, forestry, and fisheries industry group is quite different. It accounts for 6 per cent of the economy's output, but none of eleven project types requires more than 1 per cent of its gross output demands from this industry. Similarly, while nearly 30 per cent of the value of the economy's gross output occurs in the service industries, only about one-half of this percentage is required to fulfill the relative final

---

[27] It should be noted that the column of Table 7 which shows the percentage of 1958 U.S. gross output does not refer to gross national product; it refers to the nation's total output, both intermediate and final.

demands levied on the economy by the construction of eight of the twelve water resource projects.

Occupational Requirements

As with the data on production sectors, the occupational breakdown of total labor costs demonstrates substantial diversity, both among project types and between the project types and the occupational structure of the national economy. In comparisons of the different project types, several characteristics stand out. First, in all of the types except revetments and dredging, the heaviest labor demands are imposed on the occupational category composed of craftsmen, foremen, and kindred workers. Indeed, in seven of the twelve project types, over 35 per cent of total labor requirements is drawn from that major occupational group. Within that category, almost all projects place the greatest demands on the construction equipment operators. In ten of the project types, 5 per cent or more of the total labor cost is allocated to this occupation. For small earth fill dams, over 20 per cent of total labor cost is spent in this occupational category.

Ranking second from the point of view of labor demands is the broad group of operatives and kindred workers. In all save one case, 20 per cent or more of the total labor cost is spent on workers in this category; the exception is the large multiple-purpose project, with 15 per cent of labor costs allocated to this category. A consistently large suboccupation within this major group, the truck and tractor drivers, accounts for 4 per cent or more of the total labor cost in eight of the twelve project types.

When the occupational pattern of demands for water resource project construction is compared with the occupational structure within the nation, a significant disparity is noted. In six important occupational categories, the relative national labor cost far outstrips the percentage of total project labor cost. These are: professional, technical, and kindred workers; managers, officials, and proprietors; clerical and kindred workers; sales workers; service workers; and farmers and farm workers. While nationally nearly 60 per cent of total employee compensation payments goes to individuals in these categories, in ten of the twelve project types less than one-third of total labor costs can be so attributed. Conversely, while less than 25 per cent of the national labor cost arises in the three broad categories of craftsmen, foremen, and kindred workers, operatives and kindred workers, and laborers (except farm occupations), over 65 per cent of the total labor cost is paid to these occupations in ten of the project types. Even with occupations defined as broadly as in Table 7, the difference between the demands which public works construction places on the labor force and the existing structure of the labor force becomes clear.

Table 8 summarizes the disparity between the occupational requirements of the projects and the occupational composition of the U.S. labor force. There the percentage of total gross output and total employment for each project type required from those industries and occupations in which the relative project demand exceeds the relative national demand is compared with the percentage of national gross output and employment in these same industries and occupations. Typically, about 60 per cent of the gross output required for project construction is supplied by industries which produce only about 20 per cent of the nation's gross output. Stated alternatively, those industries which produce about 80 per cent of the nation's gross output supply only about 40 per cent of the gross output required for project construction. Similarly, about 40 to 45 per cent of the total labor cost for project construction is attributable to occupations which account for about 10 per cent of total labor cost nationally. In Table 8, the greater the difference between A and B for any project type, the greater the disparity between project demands and the national structure of output and employment.

The final interesting set of data produced by the model concerns the industry-by-industry breakdown of the remaining nonlabor cost components of value added—that is, net interest, depreciation, indirect business taxes, corporate profits, and proprietor and rental income. A summary of this breakdown is presented for the large multiple-purpose project in Table 9. There, many of the same patterns noted earlier are again in evidence. For example, durable goods manufacturing again absorbs a very large proportion of the total in the depreciation, indirect business taxes, and corporate profits components of value added. For net interest and proprietor and rental income, however, the situation is

Table 8. Summary of the Divergence of National Output and Employment Patterns from Detailed Project Demands

Project type	Industries which supply A % of the nation's gross output furnish B % of the gross output for project construction		Occupations which supply A % of the nation's total employment furnish B % of the total employment for project construction	
	A %	B %	A %	B %
Large earth fill dams	32	65	12	46
Small earth fill dams	32	65	13	43
Local flood protection	29	67	12	51
Pile dikes	23	59	11	49
Levees	26	47	12	51
Revetments	18	59	11	43
Powerhouse construction	18	67	9	19
Medium concrete dams	29	68	12	41
Lock and concrete dams	18	62	13	36
Large multiple-purpose projects	18	61	10	46
Dredging	21	54	6	48
Miscellaneous	34	64	9	41

Table 9. Breakdown of Nonlabor Cost Components of Value Added for the Large Multiple-Purpose Project, by Industrial Categories (in dollars per $1,000 of total contract cost)

Industrial category	Net interest	Deprecia-tion	Indirect business taxes	Corporate profits	Proprietor and rental income
Agriculture, forestry, & fisheries	.14	.63	.20	.01	1.81
Mining, including crude petroleum	.15	4.29	4.27	4.78	9.46
Construction[a]	.02	.24	.12	.15	2.27
Nondurable goods manufacturing	.13	5.46	3.61	8.36	.07
Durable goods manufacturing	.51	17.14	13.89	28.74	*
Lumber & wood products	.01	.30	.21	.38	*
Stone, clay, & glass products	.08	3.89	3.31	8.11	*
Primary metals	.13	5.85	2.21	4.71	*
Fabricated metals	.10	2.23	3.37	4.56	*
Nonelectrical machinery, except construction	.06	1.16	1.26	3.47	*
Construction machinery	.05	1.71	1.22	3.16	*
Electrical machinery	.05	1.29	1.82	3.32	*
Transportation equipment	.02	.52	.46	.75	*
Miscellaneous	.01	.20	.11	.28	*
Transportation & warehousing	.89	5.88	4.47	1.93	.44
Wholesale & retail trade	.19	3.71	11.89	4.55	6.04
Services	5.11	8.55	6.18	10.61	10.38
Total[b]	7.15	45.68	44.71	59.13	30.47

Asterisk (*) means less than $.005, but greater than zero.
[a] Refers only to maintenance and repair construction.
[b] Columns may not add because of rounding.

reversed. The services category generates over 70 per cent of total net interest payments (and within that category it is the real estate and rental industry which generates the largest net interest payment). Because of the concentration of noncorporate enterprise in the nonmanufacturing sectors of the economy, proprietor and rental income is generated primarily in the mining, wholesale and retail trade, and service sectors. In fact, these three groups of industries provide 85 per cent of the total proprietor and rental income generated by project construction.

SUMMARY AND CONCLUSIONS

The primary purpose of this chapter has been to present a method of analysis and to discuss a body of data essential for the evaluation of the social cost of public expenditures in an economy with unemployed resources. A second purpose, significant in itself, has been to investigate the structure of demands imposed on the economy by the construction of various kinds of water resource projects—demands not only for material outputs but, more particularly, demands for the primary inputs to production: labor and capital.

The accuracy of the data input on which the empirical results of this analysis depend cannot be specified with precision. Furthermore, the assumptions of the model—linearity, absence of time lags, disregard of inventory depletion as a substitute for increased production—qualify the results. Nevertheless, the exercise has both specified the mechanism by which public expenditures impose their demands on the economy and yielded detailed estimates of these demands, both industrial and occupational, for one expenditure area.

Among the broad conclusions which the analysis warrants so far are the following:

1) In considering water resource development as a stimulant for the economy, the policy maker must distinguish the several different kinds of projects. There are substantial differences in the structure of demands imposed upon the economy and each project type tends to stimulate quite different parts of the economy.

2) In addressing the needs of an economy with a given pattern of unemployment, the gross employment generated by a project is not the only relevant policy variable. Different types of projects impose their demands on widely different categories of labor.

3) In forming policy, decisions should be based on the pattern of gross output and total labor demands. Restricting information to the bills of final demand and on-site labor only lead to erroneous judgments. The indirect production and off-site labor demands generated by the bills of final demand are fully as large as the demands for direct production and on-site labor, and they form a significantly different pattern.

THE SECTORAL IMPACT OF PUBLIC INVESTMENT: A REGIONAL ANALYSIS | III

THE LABOR AND OUTPUT DEMANDS imposed on the national economy by water resource investments were estimated in substantial occupational and industrial detail in the preceding chapter. There the entire national economy was assumed to supply the required inputs. In this chapter, a regional dimension is added to the analysis. Here we estimate the occupational and industrial demands imposed on the several regions of the nation by the assumed construction of alternative types of water development projects in each of the regions.

At the outset, we should emphasize that the estimation of regional impacts is subject to less precision than the estimation of national impacts. The regional analysis requires all of the heroic assumptions of the national analysis plus a number of its own.[1] In addition to these already made, further assumptions concerning the interregional distribution of the demands *not* met by the region in which the project is built are required, as are the extent of the intraregional preference given to industries within the project region and the stability of these patterns over time, across regions, and across project types. These assumptions, in turn, imply a set of still more basic propositions concerning industrial production costs, transportation costs, brand preferences of contractors, regional trading patterns, and interregional differences in industry production functions.[2] Because knowledge on all of these matters is either extremely limited or nonexistent, whatever set of assumptions we adopt must be largely a matter of judgment. Notwithstanding the limitations, such a study is useful. While the estimates may not conform exactly to real world behavior, they will provide an analysis of regional impact based on existing knowledge where no estimates previously existed.

---

[1] See Charles M. Tiebout, "Regional and Interregional Input-Output Models: An Appraisal," *Southern Economic Journal*, Vol. 24 (October 1957), pp. 140–47. As Tiebout points out, the "empirical results of regional input-output analysis present us with a set of data which is supposed to describe reality. Unfortunately there is no alternative set of data with which the researchers' results may be compared."
[2] For an able discussion of the determinants of patterns of interregional exchange and the regional impact of an autonomous expenditure, see Walter Isard, *Methods of Regional Analysis* (Cambridge: Technology Press and John Wiley and Sons, 1960).

THE REGIONAL SECTORAL DEMAND MODEL

The regional demand model which will be used in this analysis is a modified form of the Leontief balanced regional—or, more precisely, intranational—model.[3] Our model, in estimating the regional demands imposed by a final expenditure, explicitly recognizes the fact that the outputs of some industries travel long distances in meeting required demands, while the outputs of others are consumed close to the point of production. By distinguishing the extent to which different industries satisfy the demands of users within their own region, a basis is established for allocating among regions the industrial demands imposed at a point in space. Having thus separated the various industry classes, the geographic pattern of existing industrial capacity is employed to allocate among regions the industrial demands imposed at a spatial point.

In the model, presented in detail in Appendix 4, all industries are separated into four groups—Type A, Type B, Type C, and Local industries. The type called Local includes those industries with outputs which travel only short distances from the point of production to supply the demands of local buyers. The automobile repair industry is an example. The outputs of Type A, Type B, and Type C, on the other hand, are transportable and, to a greater or less extent, move over regional boundaries.

While Local industries serve only regional users, Type A industries produce for a truly national market; these products may be produced in only one or two places in the nation but are consumed throughout the nation. Type B and Type C are intermediate to Type A and Local— they are industries whose market areas are neither local nor truly national. The outputs of these industries circulate more widely than within one narrowly defined region but not within the entire nation. Type B includes those industries lying closer to the Type A extreme; Type C more closely approximates the Local type.

It is assumed that the quantity of output produced by Local industries in a region is equal to the Local industry demand imposed in that region. Because of their supraregional characteristics, this same assumption cannot be applied to the Type A, Type B, or Type C industries. For these, a demand imposed at a spatial point is allocated among the regions on the basis of the regional distribution of industrial capacity, the category to which the industry is assigned, and a set of synthetic regional

---

[3] For a description, see Wassily Leontief *et al.*, *Studies in the Structure of the American Economy* (New York: Oxford University Press, 1953), Chaps. 3 and 4; Walter Isard and Guy Freutel, "Regional and National Product Projections and Their Interrelations," in *Long-Range Economic Projections*, National Bureau of Economic Research, Studies in Income and Wealth, Vol 16 (Princeton: Princeton University Press, 1954); and Leontief *et al.*, "The Economic Impact—Industrial and Regional—of an Arms Cut," *Review of Economics and Statistics*, Vol. 47 (August 1965), pp. 217–41.

preference functions. These functions are relationships between the relative concentration of an industry within a region and the percentage of the regionally imposed final demand for the industry's products which will be supplied by the industry's capacity within the region.

Figure 4 shows the functional relationships we adopted for allocating among the regions the final demands imposed upon each of the industry types at a spatial point. On the horizontal axis is plotted the percentage of an industry's national output produced in the region in which the demand is assumed to be imposed. On the vertical axis is plotted the proportion of the final demand for an industry's output which is allocated to the project region. Implicit in each of the functions is the proposition that the degree of regional preference shown to any industry of a region from which a final demand originates depends on the regional productive capacity of that industry relative to its national productive capacity.

In dealing with Type A industries—the truly national industries—the final demand for their output is allocated among regions in proportion to each region's contribution to the national output of the industry. If the region within which a project is located produces 20 per cent of the na-

FIGURE 4. REGIONAL PREFERENCE FUNCTIONS

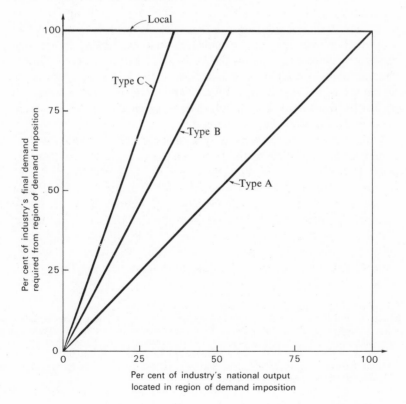

tional output of a Type A industry, 20 per cent of the final demand for the output of this industry is allocated to the project region. The remaining regions share to the extent of their participation in the national output of the industry. This relationship is depicted by the function labeled Type A in Figure 4.[4] For Type A no regional preference is shown.

For Type B and Type C industries, a distinct regional preference is assumed for the region within which the final demand is assumed to be imposed. This preference recognizes that demands imposed at a spatial point on an industry with some regional orientation will be satisfied from within the region to a greater extent than is implied by the region's contribution to the total national output of that industry. The extent of the regional preference within each of industry Types B and C is assumed to be a function of the relative concentration of the output of the industry in the project region. Hence, if project construction occurs in a region supplying 20 per cent of a Type B industry's national output, we allocate 40 per cent of the project's final demand for the outputs of this industry to the region where the project is constructed. The remaining 60 per cent is not assumed to be spatially sensitive and, therefore, is allocated among all of the regions as the entire final demand was allocated in the case of Type A industries. For a national industry classified as Type C—one bordering on the Local classification—a greater regional preference function is assumed. A project region supplying 20 per cent of a Type C industry's national ouput is allocated 60 per cent of the project's final demand for the industry's outputs. Again, the residual is distributed among regions on the basis of each region's contribution to national industry output. For industries of the Local type, the regional preference is assumed to be complete, and the entire final demand of the project for the output of such industries is assigned to the region wherein the demand is assumed to be imposed.[5]

While the regional preference functions are used to favor the project region in the allocation of the final demand of Type B and Type C industries, the indirect demands generated by the final demand are all allocated according to the rule adopted for allocating the final demand for Type A industries. All regions share the indirect demands imposed on any Type B or Type C industry in proportion to their contribution to that industry's total national output. Hence, it is assumed that purchases by contractors of direct project inputs from industries of Type B or Type C are supplied primarily from the region wherein the project is

[4] This function, it should be noted, is identical to that applied by the Leontief balanced model to all national industries—each national industry is assumed to share in supplying the gross generated output to the extent of its production as a percentage of total national production for that industry. See Leontief et al., "The Economic Impact—Industrial and Regional—of an Arms Cut," op. cit.

[5] This function is again identical to that applied by the Leontief balanced model to local industries. Leontief et al., ibid.

located. The indirect requirements from these industries is allocated among all of the regions in proportion to the region's contribution to the national production of each of these industries.[6] The indirect demands on the Local type are supplied by Local industries within the region from which the demand arises.

In structuring the model for empirical implementation, we have adopted the definition of Local industries employed in the Leontief regional analysis of decreases in defense expenditures.[7] The remaining industries are separated into Types A, B, and C on the basis of evidence regarding the extent to which the production and consumption of the outputs of these industries balance within regions of different size.[8] In general, the separation of these industries into Types A, B, and C was guided by the rather natural breaks in the empirical continuum of industries from the Local type to the truly national. Of the 80 industries whose outputs were allocable,[9] 4 are defined as Type A, 25 as Type B, 32 as Type C, and 19 as Local.

With reference to the formal model presented in Appendix 4, the computation proceeds sequentially as follows: Using as basic data the detailed final demand of the project for material, equipment, and supplies, the gross industrial requirements are estimated by accounting for the interindustry demands imposed by production sectors on each other (equation 1). Through equation 2, the gross output of the Type A industries is distributed among the regions on the basis of the geographic distribution of each industry's capacity. In equations 3, 4, and 5, the final demand of the Type B industries is allocated to the region of final demand imposition by the regional preference function; the remainder of the gross output of these industries is distributed among the regions on the basis of the geographic distribution of each industry's capacity; and the resulting allocations are aggregated to yield the regional dis-

[6] The character of Type B and Type C functions shown in Figure 4 is clearly a matter of judgment. There is no empirical evidence available to indicate what form they should take or even how many of them there should be. Nevertheless, these functions give explicit recognition of the fact that most industries are neither purely local nor purely national—that most industries demonstrate some regional preference in supplying demands imposed at a spatial point. Indeed, it should be noted that, like the intermediate functions, the extreme functions (Type A and Local) employed in the unmodified Leontief model are also based on judgment and are incapable of empirical verification. This is true even though the classification of the industries does have an empirical basis.

[7] See Leontief et al., "The Economic Impact—Industrial and Regional—of an Arms Cut," op. cit.

[8] This evidence is shown in Walter Isard's Chap. 5 in Leontief et al., Studies in the Structure of the American Economy, op. cit. The allocation of the industries into the four categories is shown in the table which makes up Appendix 7.

[9] Two industries of the eighty-two in the Office of Business Economics input-output study were not allocated as to type. Industry 80 in the list is the imports sector; the gross output demands levied on it are not regionally allocable. Industry 11 is the new construction sector and is treated as a final-demand sector in this study.

tribution of total gross outputs of the Type B industry. Equations 6, 7, and 8 perform the same function for Type C industries. The total demand imposed on a Local industry equals the final demand for the industry's output imposed in the region of project construction plus the Local industry outputs required by national industry production in each region. These demands are estimated in equations 9 and 10. In equation 11, the gross outputs of the Local industries are estimated by accounting for Local interindustry requirements.[10] Equations 12 and 13 translate the gross outputs of all of the industries, regionally distributed, into the regional distribution of off-site labor requirements, by occupation. In equations 14 and 15, the regionally distributed off-site labor costs associated with the occupational demands secured in equation 13 are estimated, adjusted, and then added to the on-site occupational labor costs (which are allocated to the region of final demand imposition) to yield the occupational labor costs for each region. A complete description of the computer process used in the computations required by the model is presented in Appendix 6.

To statistically implement this regional model only matrix H^s is required in addition to the data utilized in the national analysis of Chapter II. It consists of a 62-by-10 table of coefficients, each of which describes the fraction of a national industry's output in each of the ten regions.[11] This table of coefficients is given in Appendix 7.[12] In Table 10, the composition of each of the ten regions is shown. Empirically, this model has the following dimensional attributes: $N = 80$, $a = 4$, $b = 25$, $c = 32$, $d = 19$, $Z = 156$, $S = 10$.

ESTIMATES OF REGIONAL SECTORAL IMPACT

As in the preceding chapter, the computed results from the statistical implementation of the model appear as large and detailed tables. Here we present some of the more important of these empirical results. Other supplementary results are shown and analyzed in Appendix 10. The tables show a number of aspects of the regional distribution of the industrial gross output and occupational labor demands. For comparative

[10] It should be noted that the gross outputs for all industries estimated by the national model (Chapter II) are equal to the gross industrial outputs estimated by the regional model when summed over all the regions. That the national and regional estimates are consistent is demonstrated in Appendix 5.

[11] The majority of these coefficients were calculated from a similar 41-by-19 table prepared by the Harvard Economic Research Project. See Leontief *et al.*, "The Economic Impact—Industrial and Regional—of an Arms Cut," *op. cit.*, pp. 233–34. The remaining coefficients were calculated directly from published government data. U.S. Department of Commerce, Bureau of the Census, *Census of Manufactures, 1958.*

[12] The data contained in Appendix 7 serve as the independent variable for the regional preference functions associated with Type B and Type C industries.

Table 10. Composition of the Ten Regions Used in the Regional Sectoral Demand Model

Region number	Designation	States included in each of the ten regions
I	New England	Maine, Vermont, New Hampshire, Massachusetts, Connecticut, Rhode Island
II	Mid-Atlantic	New York, New Jersey, Pennsylvania
III	East North Central	Michigan, Ohio, Indiana, Illinois, Wisconsin
IV	West North Central	Minnesota, South Dakota, North Dakota, Iowa, Missouri, Nebraska, Kansas
V	Southeast	Georgia, North Carolina, South Carolina, Florida, Alabama, Mississippi
VI	Lower Atlantic	Virginia, West Virginia, Maryland, Delaware, District of Columbia
VII	Kentucky-Tennessee	Kentucky and Tennessee
VIII	West South Central	Oklahoma, Louisiana, Arkansas, Texas
IX	Mountain	Montana, Wyoming, Idaho, Colorado, New Mexico, Arizona, Nevada, Utah
X	West Coast	California, Oregon, Washington

purposes, a bill of final demand of the composition of the gross national product was also traced through the model and is shown in these tables.

In Table 11, the distribution among the ten regions of the gross output and labor demands of a single type of project—the large multiple-purpose project—is shown when it is assumed that the project is constructed in West Virginia in the Lower Atlantic region (VI). For comparative purposes, the regional distribution of the demands of the GNP vector is also shown, under the same set of assumptions.[13] This table presents occupational detail aggregated to 20 major occupations from the 156 detailed occupations estimated by the model, and industry data aggregated to 17 major production sectors from the 82 detailed industries for which the model yielded estimates. In addition, while only the results for one project type assumed to be constructed in a single region are shown in the table, the implementation of the model yielded estimates for all twelve project types, and each type was assumed to be constructed in each of the ten regions.

Of the total gross output of $1,032 (per $1,000 of contract cost)

---

[13] In implementing the GNP vector for bench-mark purposes, the final-output demand vector used was just sufficient in size to yield a sum of gross outputs equal to that of the large multiple-purpose project—that is, $1,032. While both final-demand vectors generated $1,032 in gross industrial output, the sum of final demands of the project vector was $514, while the GNP vector summed across industries to $523. While the bench-mark vector is referred to as the GNP vector in the study, its composition differs from the composition of the gross national product in one significant way. In the bench-mark vector, the final demand for the new construction industry was eliminated. Such exclusion seems appropriate because it is a new construction expenditure which is being compared with a more general pattern of final demand.

Table 11. The Large Multiple-Purpose Project and Gross National Product[a] in the Lower Atlantic Region: Allocation of Gross Output by Industry and Labor Cost by Occupation[b] to Ten Regions (in dollars per $1,000 of total contract cost and per cent of total national gross output required)

Category	I New England				II Mid-Atlantic				III East North Central				IV West North Central				V Southeast			
	Project		GNP		Project		GNP		Project		GNP		Project		GNP		Project		GNP	
	$	%	$	%	$	%	$	%	$	%	$	%	$	%	$	%	$	%	$	%
Industry																				
Agriculture, forestry, & fisheries	*	5	2	3	*	6	4	6	1	15	12	17	2	21	18	25	1	13	8	11
Mining, including crude petroleum	*	**	*	**	4	5	1	6	4	5	2	7	4	6	1	7	1	2	1	3
Construction	*	2	*	1	1	11	1	3	1	16	1	4	*	3	1	2	*	2	*	2
Nondurable goods manufacturing	7	7	16	7	20	20	53	21	24	23	46	18	5	5	17	7	7	7	26	10
Durable goods manufacturing	31	6	15	7	126	23	46	22	197	37	78	38	27	5	10	5	20	4	7	4
Lumber & wood products	1	5	1	5	1	7	1	12	1	12	2	18	1	4	*	4	5	13	2	14
Stone, clay, & glass products	4	5	*	3	15	19	2	28	19	24	2	28	6	8	*	5	5	7	*	7
Primary metals	6	4	2	5	37	28	9	29	47	36	11	36	4	3	1	3	5	4	1	3
Fabricated metals	6	6	2	9	23	23	4	23	31	31	7	40	6	3	1	5	5	5	1	2
Nonelectrical machinery, except construction	8	10	3	11	22	29	7	24	34	45	12	43	3	4	2	7	1	1	1	2
Construction machinery	1	1	*	1	4	8	*	8	27	52	12	52	4	7	*	7	1	2	*	2
Electrical machinery	5	8	3	9	19	29	8	30	26	40	10	36	3	5	1	4	1	2	1	2
Transportation equipment	4	3	3	4	3	14	8	13	11	52	28	44	1	4	4	6	4	4	2	3
Miscellaneous	1	14	2	15	3	45	6	42	1	21	3	22	*	5	1	5	*	2	*	3
Transportation & warehousing	1	2	1	2	6	8	3	8	8	11	4	10	2	2	1	3	1	2	1	3
Wholesale & retail trade	1	2	1	1	6	6	4	3	9	9	5	4	1	2	2	1	1	2	2	1
Services	4	3	3	1	14	11	11	4	21	16	14	5	4	3	5	2	3	2	4	1
Total gross output required[c]	45		39		177		123		264		162		45		56		36		49	
Per cent of total national gross output required	4		4		17		12		26		16		4		5		3		5	

Occupation										
Professional, technical, & kindred workers	2	1	6	3	9	4	1	1	1	1
Managers, officials, & proprietors	1	1	5	3	8	3	1	1	1	1
Clerical & kindred workers	2	1	6	3	9	4	1	1	1	1
Sales workers	*	*	1	1	1	1	*	*	*	*
Craftsmen, foremen, & kindred workers	3	2	11	5	18	6	3	3	2	1
Carpenters	*	*	*	*	*	*	*	*	*	*
Cement finishers	*	*	*	*	*	*	*	*	*	*
Iron & metal workers	*	*	*	*	*	*	*	*	*	*
Construction equipment operators	*	*	1	*	1	1	*	*	*	*
Other building trades	*	*	1	*	3	1	*	*	*	*
Mechanics	1	*	2	1	4	1	1	1	*	*
Labor foremen	1	1	2	1	4	1	1	1	1	*
Others	1	1	5	2	9	2	1	1	1	1
Operatives & kindred workers	4	3	13	9	20	9	3	2	3	3
Truck & tractor drivers	*	*	2	1	2	1	1	*	1	*
Sailors & deck hands	*	*	*	*	*	*	*	*	*	*
Others	3	2	12	7	17	8	2	2	2	3
Service workers	*	*	1	1	2	1	*	*	*	*
Laborers	1	*	3	1	4	1	1	1	1	1
Farmers & farm workers	*	*	*	*	*	2	*	3	*	2
Total labor cost[c]	12	9	47	26	70	31	12	11	10	10
Per cent of total national labor cost	2	4	7	10	10	12	2	4	1	4

One asterisk (*) means less than $.50 but greater than zero; two (**) mean less than .5 per cent but greater than zero.

[a] For the meaning of the data in the GNP columns and their relationship to the project data, see footnote 13 in Chapter III.

[b] The labor costs for the project given in the table under Region VI are broken down as follows: on-site labor cost + off-site labor cost = total labor cost for each occupational category within the region and for total labor cost. Similarly, this same breakdown of costs into on-site, off-site, and total labor for the project is given in the last column showing total national labor costs.

[c] Rows may not add because of rounding.

Table 11. (Continued)

Category	VI Lower Atlantic: location of project Project $	%	GNP $	%	VII Kentucky-Tennessee Project $	%	GNP $	%	VIII West South Central Project $	%	GNP $	%	IX Mountain Project $	%	GNP $	%	X West Coast Project $	%	GNP $	%	United States Project $	GNP $
Industry																						
Agriculture, forestry, & fisheries	*	4	3	4	*	3	2	3	1	13	9	12	1	6	5	7	1	15	9	12	8	74
Mining, including crude petroleum	45	58	2	10	1	2	1	3	10	14	10	45	5	6	3	12	2	3	2	7	77	22
Construction	5	54	19	82	*	1	*	1	*	4	1	2	*	2	*	1	*	4	*	2	9	23
Nondurable goods manufacturing	11	11	40	16	3	3	8	3	14	14	20	8	2	2	4	2	9	8	20	8	103	248
Durable goods manufacturing	49	9	12	6	9	2	3	1	25	5	6	3	13	2	4	2	43	8	24	12	539	205
Lumber & wood products	1	8	1	13	*	3	*	3	1	7	1	6	1	5	*	3	5	35	3	23	13	12
Stone, clay, & glass products	13	17	1	10	2	3	*	2	5	6	*	5	2	3	*	3	7	9	1	9	78	7
Primary metals	14	11	2	7	1	1	1	1	3	3	1	3	7	5	2	7	7	5	2	6	129	30
Fabricated metals	12	12	1	4	3	3	*	2	5	5	1	4	1	1	*	1	10	10	2	10	100	18
Nonelectrical machinery, except construction	2	2	1	3	*	1	*	2	1	1	1	2	*	**	*	1	4	5	2	7	75	29
Construction machinery	2	3	*	3	1	1	*	1	9	17	1	17	1	2	*	*	3	7	*	7	52	4
Electrical machinery	3	5	1	5	1	5	1	2	1	1	*	1	*	**	*	**	5	8	2	9	64	27
Transportation equipment	1	7	4	7	*	1	*	1	1	3	2	3	*	**	1	1	2	10	11	18	20	63
Miscellaneous	*	2	*	2	*	1	*	1	*	2	*	2	*	1	*	1	*	6	1	6	7	15
Transportation & warehousing	49	58	27	63	1	1	*	1	2	3	2	4	1	1	1	1	2	3	2	4	72	43
Wholesale & retail trade	70	75	108	85	1	1	1	**	2	2	1	1	1	1	1	**	2	2	2	2	93	126
Services	71	54	239	82	1	1	2	1	6	5	6	2	2	2	2	1	5	4	6	2	131	291
Total gross output required[c]	300		450		16		16		61		54		24		19		65		65		1,032	1,032
Per cent of total national gross output required	29		44		2		2		6		5		2		2		6		6			

46

Occupation	On-site +off-site =total										On-site +off-site =total	
Professional, technical, & kindred workers	39+ 10 = 49	9	26	19	*	2	1	1	*	2	2	39+ 34 = 72	41
Managers, officials, & proprietors	20+ 23 = 43	8	29	21	1	2	1	1	*	2	1	20+ 46 = 66	41
Clerical & kindred workers	5+ 17 = 22	4	24	17	1	2	1	1	*	2	2	5+ 41 = 46	37
Sales workers	0+ 6 = 6	1	9	6	*	*	*	*	*	*	*	*+ 10 = 10	11
Craftsmen, foremen, & kindred workers	253+ 21 =274	52	20	14	1	3	1	1	1	4	2	253+ 66 =319	40
Carpenters	47+ 1 = 48	19	2	1	*	*	*	*	*	*	*	47+ 2 = 49	2
Cement finishers	4+ 0 = 4	1	*	*	*	*	*	*	*	*	*	4+ * = 4	*
Iron & metal workers	22+ 0 = 22	4	*	*	*	*	*	*	*	*	*	22+ 1 = 22	1
Construction equipment operators	43+ 2 = 45	9	*	*	*	*	*	*	*	*	*	43+ 4 = 48	1
Other building trades	35+ 2 = 37	7	3	2	*	*	*	*	*	*	*	35+ 6 = 41	5
Mechanics	5+ 7 = 12	2	7	5	*	*	*	*	*	1	*	5+ 13 = 18	10
Labor foremen	45+ 3 = 48	9	2	1	*	1	*	*	*	1	*	45+ 13 = 58	6
Others	52+ 6 = 58	11	6	4	*	1	*	*	*	2	1	52+ 36 = 88	15
Operatives & kindred workers	28+ 26 = 54	10	16	11	1	3	2	2	1	5	3	28+ 80 =108	49
Truck & tractor drivers	8+ 7 = 15	3	4	3	*	1	*	*	*	1	*	8+ 14 = 22	7
Sailors & deck hands	*+ *= *	*	*	*	*	*	*	*	*	*	*	*+ * = *	*
Others	20+ 19 = 39	7	12	9	1	3	1	1	1	4	2	20+ 66 = 86	42
Service workers	0+ 3 = 3	1	12	9	*	*	*	*	*	*	*	0+ 7 = 7	14
Laborers	72+ 5 = 77	15	5	4	*	1	*	*	*	1	1	72+ 17 = 89	11
Farmers & farm workers	*+ *= *	*	1	1	*	*	2	*	*	*	2	*+ 2 = 2	13
Total labor cost[c]	416+111 =527	140	54	4	3	13	8	6	4	18	14	416+303 =719	257
Per cent of total national labor cost	73				1	2	3	1	2	3	5		

generated by the final demand of the large multiple-purpose project, 29 per cent ($300) is supplied from industries in the Lower Atlantic region. Because of the relative paucity of regional capacity in those national industries upon which project construction most heavily draws, nearly two-thirds of the output stimulated in this region occurs in the categories of wholesale and retail trade, transportation and warehousing, and services—all of them the Local type of industry. On the other hand, because of the extremely heavy concentration of durable goods manufacturing in the Mid-Atlantic and East North Central regions (II and III), over 40 per cent of the total gross output requirements are supplied by these two regions—even though the project is constructed in Region VI. That it is durable goods manufacturing which accounts for this result is evident from the table. Of the total gross output of $1,032, durable goods accounted for $539; of this value, $325, or 60 per cent occurred in Regions II and III. Taken together, three regions—Mid-Atlantic, East North Central, and Lower Atlantic—account for over 70 per cent of total gross output requirements.

In comparing this regional distribution of gross output with the distribution generated by a final demand of the composition of the gross national product, a number of significant differences are evident. As seen in the total gross output column, while over 50 per cent of the gross output demands called forth by the project are concentrated in durable goods manufacturing, only about 20 per cent of the gross demands generated by the GNP vector are so concentrated. For the GNP final-demand vector, the concentration of demands is found in nondurable goods and services, which contain 25 per cent and 29 per cent of total gross output requirements. Because of the diversity in the industrial pattern of gross output demands of these two vectors, the impact on the regions varies significantly. While because of the Lower Atlantic region's small capacity of durable goods industries, Region VI supplies 29 per cent of the gross output demands of the large multiple-purpose project, 44 per cent of the gross demands of the GNP vector are supplied from this region. Conversely, because of the relatively smaller durable goods requirements of the GNP vector, those regions which are heavy suppliers of durable goods receive a smaller impact from this vector than from the water project vector. Hence, while the impact of the water resource project on Regions II and III, taken together, amounted to 43 per cent of the total gross output, the impact was only 28 per cent of the equivalent GNP vector.

These patterns are even more noticeable when individual industry groupings are investigated. For mining (including crude petroleum), while the Lower Atlantic region retained nearly 60 per cent of the gross output requirement for project construction, it retained only 10 per cent of the total gross output generated by the GNP vector. The opposite occurs in the West South Central region. This region was allocated only

14 per cent of mining's gross output in the case of the water resource expenditure, but 45 per cent for the GNP vector.

A comparison of the regional distributions for durable and nondurable goods manufacturing shows no significant variation of the percentage patterns among regions, but because of the large absolute differences in the industry's gross output in the two vectors, the dollar impacts are quite diverse. For example, the impact from nondurable goods in the Lower Atlantic region was $40 from the GNP vector, compared to an impact of $11 from the water resource project. As another example, the impact of durable goods in Regions II and III together was $325 from the water resource project and $124 from the GNP vector. Analysis of the patterns in services and in wholesale and retail trade is also revealing. Because most of the industries in these sectors are of the Local type, the high relative demands of the GNP vector on these sectors are largely retained in the region in which the final demand is assumed to be imposed. Thus, while the Lower Atlantic region supplied $141 of gross output from services and trade to the water resource project, it supplied nearly $350 of gross output in these two categories to the GNP vector.

In the lower portion of Table 11, the regional allocation of the total labor cost, by occupation, is shown for both the large multiple-purpose project and for the GNP vector generating an equivalent gross output, on the assumption that both of the final demands are imposed in the Lower Atlantic region. The earlier description of the formal model pointed out that the total labor cost generated by the final demand is composed of both on-site and off-site demands. These two components are allocated among the ten regions on the basis of substantially different assumptions. In the case of on-site labor, it is assumed that the entire demand is drawn from the region wherein the project is located. Off-site labor demands depend upon the regional allocation of the gross industrial output. Consequently, off-site demands are imposed in some pattern on all of the ten regions no matter where the project is assumed to be located. On-site demands are imposed on the project region alone. (These assumptions are incorporated in equations 11 through 15 of the formal model.)

In contrast to the 29 per cent of total gross output stimulated by the water resource project which is supplied by the Lower Atlantic region in which the final demand is imposed, $527 or 73 per cent of the total labor cost of $719 is allocated to that project region.[14] This is composed of $416 of on-site and $111 of off-site labor costs. As implied by the evidence on the regional allocation of gross output requirements, the Mid-Atlantic and East North Central regions (II with 7 per cent and

---

[14] In comparing the structure of occupational demands imposed by the two final-demand vectors, the GNP pattern must be contrasted with the off-site figures in the column for the Lower Atlantic region and in the final column.

III with 10 per cent) supply the bulk of the labor demands for the water resource project not retained in the Lower Atlantic region. Thus when the construction of the large multiple-purpose project is assumed to be in the Lower Atlantic region, 90 per cent of total labor costs are concentrated in Regions II, III, and VI. Only one other region—the West Coast—supplies as much as $18 or 3 per cent of the total labor demanded.

Not unexpectedly, the project's occupational labor demands that are concentrated within the Lower Atlantic region vary substantially about the 73 per cent figure for total labor costs. For example, while 86 per cent of the total labor cost for the major category of craftsmen, foremen, and kindred workers is retained within the Lower Atlantic region, only 50 per cent of the cost attributable to the category of operative and kindred workers is retained. For the detailed occupational categories, the distribution of labor cost retained in the region of final demand varies from 4 to 99 per cent.

When comparing the pattern of labor demands generated by the water resource project and the GNP vectors, a number of significant differences appear. While the gross output of $1,032 for the GNP vector generates $257 of off-site labor cost, the equivalent water resource project vector requires $303, or almost 20 per cent more off-site labor cost. The public project tends to draw on industries which are relatively more labor intensive than the industries drawn on by the final demand of the composition of the gross national product. In the individual occupational categories, the main differences occur in the major categories of craftsmen, foremen, and kindred workers, the operatives and kindred workers, the service workers, and the farmers and farm workers. In the first two of these four categories, the water resource project imposes greater demands than does the GNP vector ($66 compared to $40 and $80 to $49, respectively). In the latter two categories, the GNP vector imposes significantly greater demands than does the final demand vector for the project (services with $14 for the GNP vector compared to $7 for the project, and farming $13 compared to $2).

The pattern changes for off-site labor demands retained within the region in which the final expenditure is assumed to be made. Whereas the total off-site labor expense generated by the project is significantly greater than the GNP vector, in the region where construction takes place, the GNP vector imposes $140 of labor requirements compared to $111 for the water project. In individual occupational categories, substantial differences are also noted. In the Lower Atlantic region, the GNP vector requirement for professional, technical, and kindred workers is more than double that of the water resource project; and the GNP vector requires significantly larger quantities in the categories of managers, officials, and proprietors ($29 compared to $23), clerical and kindred workers ($24 to $17), sales workers ($9 to $6), and service workers ($12 to $3). Conversely, the project's off-site labor demands on the Lower Atlantic region are drawn in greater quantities from the category of operatives and kindred workers ($26 to $16).

The regional distribution of labor demands not retained in the region where the project is constructed is directly comparable to the totals given in the final row of Table 11. As noted earlier, the water resource project's large demand for durable goods is to a significant extent exported from the region where the demand is imposed (except in a case where demand might be imposed on Regions II or III). Because of this exported demand and the GNP vector's concentration of demands in the locally oriented service industries, the total labor demand for the GNP vector is relatively more concentrated in the Lower Atlantic region than is that of the water resource project. Thus, while the water project in Region VI exports $117 of labor demand to Regions II and III, the GNP vector exports $57, or less than one-half as much. Of this difference, much is accounted for by the craftsmen, foremen, and kindred workers.

While Table 11 shows how output and employment changes in each of the regions when the large multiple-purpose project is constructed in the Lower Atlantic region, Table 12 permits a comparison of the effects on that region if additional types of projects were also constructed there. The swamping effect of the industries which are defined as Type C or Local is unmistakable. For all types of projects, mining (including crude petroleum), transportation and warehousing, wholesale and retail trade, and service categories (all of which are Type C or Local industries) account for over 60 per cent of the total gross output impact in Region VI. For the GNP final-demand vector, these industries account for over 80 per cent of the total gross output retained in the region. While from 24 to 32 per cent of total gross output generated by water project construction is retained in Region VI, 44 per cent of the gross output generated by the GNP vector is so retained.

Of significance in the second part of Table 12 is the wide disparity among project types in the pattern of occupational labor demands imposed on the region. While the total labor impact on the Lower Atlantic region varies within the $424 to $527 range, the variation of individual occupational categories is far larger. For example, the labor demand for craftsmen, foremen, and kindred workers extends from nearly $80 to about three and a half times that amount. Similarly, the demand for operatives and kindred workers extends from almost $55 to over $145.

Finally, it should be noted that for each of the projects shown (and also for the remaining types not shown in Table 12), well over two-thirds of the total employment impact is retained in the Lower Atlantic region. This compares with 54 per cent retained in the region for the GNP vector. In part, this difference is attributable to our decision to allocate all on-site labor costs to the region in which the project is as-

Table 12. Five Representative Project Types and Gross National Product in the Lower Atlantic Region: Allocation of Gross Output by Industry and Labor Cost by Occupation to the Region of Project Location (in dollars per $1,000 of total contract cost and per cent of totals)

Categories	Large earth fill dams	Local flood protection	Medium concrete dams	Dredging	Large multiple-purpose projects	GNP[a]	Range for projects
Industry							
Agriculture, forestry, & fisheries	*	*	*	*	*	3	*_*
Mining, including crude petroleum	3	44	6	3	45	2	3–45
Construction	4	5	5	4	5	19	4–5
Nondurable goods manufacturing	19	10	12	16	11	40	10–19
Durable goods manufacturing	28	46	57	79	49	12	28–79
Lumber & wood products	1	2	1	*	1	1	*_2
Stone, clay, & glass products	4	15	21	1	13	1	1–21
Primary metals	6	7	14	16	14	2	6–16
Fabricated metals	9	19	13	2	12	1	2–19
Nonelectrical machinery, except construction	1	*	2	*	2	1	*_2
Construction machinery	4	1	3	1	2	*	1–4
Electrical machinery	*	*	1	*	2	1	*_3
Transportation equipment	4	1	3	57	1	4	1–57
Miscellaneous	*	*	*	*	*	*	*_*
Transportation & warehousing	23	48	28	25	49	27	23–49
Wholesale & retail trade	121	91	91	63	70	108	63–121
Services	74	75	89	62	71	239	62–89
Total gross output required[b]	272	321	288	251	300	450	251–321
Per cent of national gross output	24	32	26	26	29	44	24–32

Occupation							
Professional, technical, & kindred workers	35	24	49	37	49	26	24–49
Managers, officials, & proprietors	37	40	37	122	43	29	37–122
Clerical & kindred workers	24	23	21	18	22	24	18–24
Sales workers	9	7	7	5	6	9	5–9
Craftsmen, foremen, & kindred workers	173	235	194	78	274	20	78–274
Carpenters	19	46	31	2	48	2	2–48
Cement finishers	3	10	4	*	4	*	*–10
Iron & metal workers	3	29	17	1	22	*	1–29
Construction equipment operators	51	82	34	5	45	*	5–82
Other building trades	3	3	25	5	37	3	3–37
Mechanics	25	16	9	9	12	7	9–25
Labor foremen	23	33	28	9	48	2	9–48
Others	46	16	46	47	58	6	16–58
Operatives & kindred workers	98	90	79	146	54	16	54–146
Truck & tractor drivers	53	44	19	4	15	4	4–53
Sailors & deckhands	*	*	*	68	*	*	*–68
Others	45	46	60	74	39	12	39–74
Service workers	3	3	3	11	3	12	3–11
Laborers	45	78	73	44	77	5	44–78
Farmers & farm workers	*	*	*	*	*	1	*–*
Total labor cost[b]	424	500	463	461	527	140	424–527
Per cent of national labor cost	69	75	69	73	73	54	69–75

Asterisk (*) means less than $.50 but greater than zero.
[a] For the meaning of the data in the GNP column and their relationship to the project data, see footnote 13 in Chapter III.
[b] Columns may not add because of rounding.

sumed to be constructed. The higher concentration of local industry final demands in the GNP vector also helps to explain this pattern.

Table 13 again focuses on the large multiple-purpose project. In this case, however, the project is assumed to be shifted sequentially among each of the ten regions, and the industrial gross output and occupational

Table 13. The Large Multiple-Purpose Project and Gross National Product[a] in Each of Ten Regions: Allocation of Gross Output by Industry and Labor Cost by Occupation to Region of Project Location (in dollars per $1,000 of total contract cost and per cent of total)

Categories	I New England Project	GNP	II Mid-Atlantic Project	GNP	III East North Central Project	GNP
Industry						
Agriculture, forestry, & fisheries	*	3	*	6	1	17
Mining, including crude petroleum	42	*	47	2	48	2
Construction	5	19	7	20	7	21
Nondurable goods manufacturing	13	46	34	127	40	116
Durable goods manufacturing	73	29	278	76	379	112
Lumber & wood products	1	1	2	4	3	5
Stone, clay, & glass products	14	*	46	2	57	2
Primary metals	9	2	61	10	70	12
Fabricated metals	16	2	69	6	82	9
Nonelectrical machinery, except construction	16	6	42	13	55	20
Construction machinery	2	*	11	1	48	3
Electrical machinery	13	5	39	14	49	17
Transportation equipment	1	5	4	14	12	36
Miscellaneous	2	6	4	11	2	7
Transportation & warehousing	49	28	58	32	62	34
Wholesale & retail trade	71	109	80	114	84	115
Services	72	238	94	254	104	257
Total gross output required[b]	326	472	599	632	724	675
Per cent of total national gross output required	32	46	58	61	70	65
Occupation						
Professional, technical, & kindred workers	50		59		64	
Managers, officials, & proprietors	44		53		58	
Clerical & kindred workers	23		32		37	
Sales workers	6		7		8	
Craftsmen, foremen, & kindred workers	275		293		302	
Carpenters	48		48		48	
Cement finishers	4		4		4	
Iron & metal workers	22		22		22	
Construction equipment operators	45		46		46	
Other building trades	37		39		39	
Mechanics	12		14		16	
Labor foremen	49		53		54	
Others	58		67		73	
Operatives & kindred workers	56		77		87	
Truck & tractor drivers	15		19		20	
Sailors & deck hands	*		*		*	
Others	41		58		67	
Service workers	3		5		5	
Laborers	77		82		84	
Farmers & farm workers	*		*		*	
Total labor cost[b]	534		608		645	
On-site labor cost as per cent of total labor cost[c]	78		68		64	
Per cent of total national labor cost	74		85		90	

Asterisk (*) means less than $.50 but greater than zero.
[a] For the meaning of the data in the GNP columns and their relationship to the project data, see footnote 13 in Chapter III.

labor impact on each of the regions in which the project is assumed to be constructed are shown.

As expected, the Mid-Atlantic (II) and East North Central (III) regions retain a higher proportion of the gross output within the region than do the other regions. When the large multiple-purpose project is

IV West North Central		V Southeast		VI Lower Atlantic		VII Kentucky-Tennessee		VIII West South Central		IX Mountain		X West Coast	
Project	GNP	Project	GNP	Project	GNP	Project	GNP	Project	GNP	Project	GNP	Project	GNP
2	25	1	13	*	3	*	3	1	13	1	8	1	13
47	2	44	1	45	2	43	1	53	10	47	3	45	2
5	20	5	20	5	19	5	19	5	20	5	19	5	20
11	60	13	64	11	40	8	33	26	54	6	22	17	63
76	19	58	14	49	12	26	6	70	12	30	6	110	40
1	1	3	4	1	1	1	1	2	2	1	1	8	5
21	*	19	1	13	1	8	*	18	1	8	*	25	1
7	1	9	1	14	2	3	*	6	1	10	2	11	2
21	1	18	1	12	1	10	1	18	1	6	*	34	3
6	4	2	1	2	1	2	1	2	1	*	*	7	4
10	1	2	*	2	*	1	*	22	2	3	*	9	1
8	2	3	1	3	1	1	1	1	1	1	*	12	5
1	6	1	4	1	4	*	1	1	4	*	1	3	18
1	2	*	1	*	*	*	*	*	1	*	*	1	2
50	29	50	28	49	27	48	27	51	29	48	27	51	29
71	110	70	109	70	108	69	107	71	108	69	107	72	110
74	240	72	239	71	239	68	235	76	240	69	234	77	248
335	504	313	488	300	450	266	431	353	487	274	426	379	525
32	49	30	47	29	44	26	42	34	47	27	41	37	51
50		49		49		48		50		48		52	
45		44		43		44		45		43		47	
23		23		22		21		24		21		25	
6		6		6		6		6		6		6	
276		274		274		271		276		272		279	
48		48		48		48		48		48		48	
4		4		4		4		4		4		4	
22		22		22		22		22		22		22	
45		45		45		45		45		43		45	
37		37		37		37		37		37		37	
12		12		12		11		12		11		12	
49		49		48		48		49		48		49	
59		57		58		56		59		59		62	
57		56		54		52		56		52		61	
16		16		15		15		16		15		16	
*		*		*		*		*		*		*	
41		40		39		37		40		37		45	
3		3		3		3		3		3		3	
78		78		77		77		78		77		79	
*		*		*		*		*		*		*	
538		533		527		522		538		522		552	
77		78		79		80		77		80		75	
75		74		73		73		75		73		77	

b Columns may not add because of rounding.

c This is the percentage of total labor cost retained in the region which is accounted for by the $416 of on-site labor cost for the large multiple-purpose project shown in Table 11.

assumed to be located in each, Region II retains 58 per cent of the gross output demands and Region III retains 70 per cent. Because of the different patterns of final demand in the two regions, the percentages, respectively, are 61 and 65 for the GNP vector. The significantly lower final demand for durable goods output in the GNP vector explains the decrease in gross output retained in Region III, the heavy supplier of such outputs. Contrasted with the significant proportion of total gross output stimulated by the multiple-purpose project which is retained in Regions II and III is the relative inability of the remaining eight regions to retain a sizable share of the generated output when the final demand is assumed to be imposed in them. In fact, the range in the remaining regions is from 26 per cent in the Kentucky-Tennessee region to 37 per cent in the West Coast region. Again, it is the distribution of the durable goods manufacturing industries which produces this result. While Regions II and III, as regions of demand imposition, retain $278 and $379 respectively out of the total durable goods output of $539 required for the project (as shown in Table 7), the next highest amount is $110 retained by the West Coast, and amounts in the other regions vary to a low of $26 in the Kentucky-Tennessee region.

The disparity among regions in the ability to retain gross outputs when final demands are imposed within their bounds is significantly smaller for the GNP vector than for the multiple-purpose project. The percentage range for the GNP vector is from 41 per cent in Region IX (the Mountain region) to 65 per cent in Region III, as compared with that of 26 per cent retained in Region VII to 70 per cent retained in Region III. This result is explained by the lower percentage of the geographically concentrated durable goods output in the gross output pattern of the GNP vector than that of the project vector, together with the significantly higher proportion of gross outputs in the Local industry sectors in the GNP vector.

By comparing the disparity among individual industry outputs retained in a region, the importance of a region's industrial structure in affecting the regional allocation of outputs can be examined. For example, for both vectors, the East North Central region (III) retains a significantly greater proportion of the gross generated outputs than does the West South Central region (VIII); yet in mining (including crude petroleum), Region VIII retains $53 of the project's gross output while Region III retains but $48, and Region VIII retains $10 of GNP gross output while Region III retains but $2. This is explained by the overwhelming proportion of the national crude oil production located in Region VIII. Similarly, the Mid-Atlantic region, because of its concentrated primary metals industry, retains $61 of this industry's gross output while Region VIII retains but $6.

In the lower portion of Table 13, similar divergences for labor costs appear as the large multiple-purpose project is shifted among regions.

Because of the ability of the Mid-Atlantic (II) and East North Central (III) regions to retain a sizable share of the durable goods output generated by project construction, the percentage of total national labor costs retained within these regions is also substantial. Each of these regions retains in excess of $600, or 85 per cent, of the total national labor costs generated by $1,000 of project construction. On the other hand, the median percentage retained by the remaining eight regions is 74 per cent. This situation is reflected in the percentage of the total labor cost retained which is accounted for by the on-site labor cost component (all of which is allocated to the project region). While on-site labor costs are 68 per cent and 64 per cent of the total labor costs retained in Regions II and III, they account for 75 per cent to 80 per cent of the total retained in the eight other regions.

Figures 5 and 6 show the regional impact on gross output and labor cost from construction of the large multiple-purpose project and the imposition of an equivalent demand of the composition of GNP. The first of these maps, which summarizes details given in Table 11, displays the impact on each region when the final demand of the project and GNP is imposed on the Lower Atlantic region. The second, based on Table 13, portrays the impact on each region when the two final demands are imposed on it.

The extent to which each of the project types has an impact on the region in which it is located (or, conversely, the extent to which it exports demands to an area far from the construction site), is shown in Table 14. The columns labeled A show the gross output remaining in the region of final demand imposition by region and project type. The range of effects on gross output in each region when the project construction takes place in each of the other regions is shown in column B.

The A columns reveal some striking differences. Comparison of the revetments and powerhouse construction projects illustrate this. While no region of project construction retained less than $800 of gross output, or 59 per cent of the total generated by the construction of revetments, only two of the ten regions retained so great a share for powerhouse construction. The median percentage retained was 61.5 per cent for revetments but only 19.5 per cent for powerhouse construction. In general, those types of installations in which the unit project cost is relatively low—such as pile dikes, levees, and revetments—tend to be substantially more regionally oriented than are the project types requiring large and more capital-intensive structures. This is shown by the median percentages of total gross output retained in the region of final demand appearing at the bottom of the table. Again, overwhelming geographical concentration of the durable goods industries in Regions II and III—because these industries are significant input suppliers to the larger projects—mainly explains this phenomenon. Although it is not shown in Table 14, the gross output pattern for final demands of

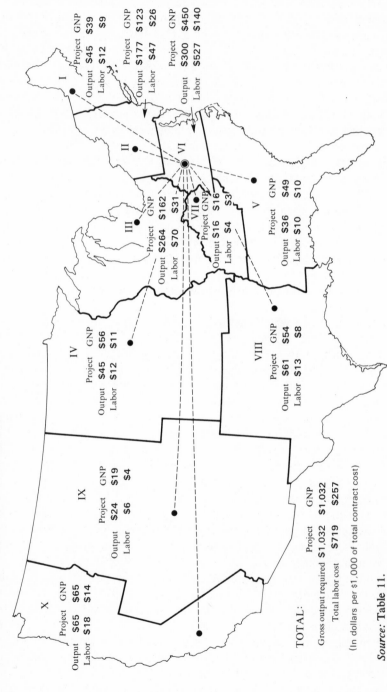

FIGURE 5. SUMMARY OF REGIONAL IMPACT OF THE LARGE MULTIPLE-PURPOSE PROJECT AND GNP WHEN FINAL DEMANDS ARE IMPOSED IN THE LOWER ATLANTIC REGION

Source: Table 11.

FIGURE 6. SUMMARY OF IMPACT ON TEN REGIONS WHEN FINAL DEMANDS FOR THE LARGE MULTIPLE-PURPOSE PROJECT AND GNP ARE IMPOSED IN EACH

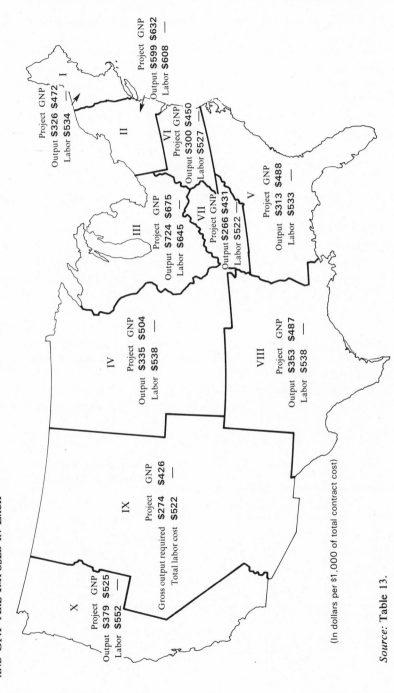

(In dollars per $1,000 of total contract cost)

Source: Table 13.

the GNP vector is significantly more regionally oriented than all the project types except pile dikes and revetments.

While some of the projects are rather strongly oriented to the region where final demand is imposed because of the types of inputs required, some regions are able to retain a larger proportion of the gross output generated by project construction within their borders because of the pattern of their productive capability. This can also be seen in Table 14. Regions II and III in no case retain less than $430 or 45 per cent of the total gross output generated when the final demand is imposed within their bounds. While this is in part accounted for by the sheer size of their productive capacity, it is in large measure due to the industrial structure of this capacity. By contrast, Regions I, IV, V, VI, VII, and IX only retain as much as 40 per cent of the gross output in the regionally oriented revetments category. These differences are reflected in the median regional percentages shown in the final column of the table: Region II and III medians are 54 and 66 per cent, respectively, while median estimates for the remaining eight regions range from 25 per cent in Region VII to 40 per cent in Region VIII.

As noted earlier, the differences in production impact on each region from project types which are assumed to be constructed in all other regions are summarized in the columns labeled *B* in the table. For example, the intersection of the West Coast row and column *B* for levees states that the shifting of levee construction among Regions I through IX requires gross output from Region X ranging from $33 to $47. Further inspection of the table will reveal the extent of such variation. When the variation caused by alternative project types is added to the variation caused by constructing the project types in alternative regions, signifi-

Table 14. Twelve Project Types in Ten Regions: (A) Gross Output Retained in Each Region of Project Location, and (B) Range of Gross Output Allocated to Region as Project Is Shifted Among Remaining Regions (in dollars per $1,000 of total contract cost)

	Region	Large earth fill dams		Small earth fill dams		Local flood protection		Pile dikes		Levees		Revetments	
		A	B	A	B	A	B	A	B	A	B	A	B
I	New England	285	27–36	344	29–38	340	25–37	486	28–36	321	16–21	844	26–29
II	Mid-Atlantic	513	108–157	586	119–168	577	94–152	594	84–107	437	65–85	927	80–91
III	East North Central	753	286–335	866	322–371	711	184–242	713	162–186	544	134–163	1,010	134–147
IV	West North Central	319	30–49	382	33–54	371	26–45	475	26–34	338	20–29	844	27–31
V	Southeast	285	25–35	344	28–38	350	24–39	486	31–39	313	15–19	857	27–34
VI	Lower Atlantic	272	22–30	344	26–35	321	21–31	464	24–30	313	14–17	830	21–23
VII	Kentucky-Tennessee	251	11–16	318	13–19	299	10–17	443	11–13	297	7–8	816	10–12
VIII	West South Central	456	86–126	535	85–133	412	50–75	562	65–86	478	85–113	940	84–97
IX	Mountain	274	20–26	331	21–27	309	17–24	454	18–21	313	14–18	830	18–21
X	West Coast	377	49–75	433	50–77	433	42–70	572	69–85	379	33–47	927	67–76
Median percentage of total gross output retained		26.5		28.5		35		45		40		61.5	

cant variations in the demands imposed on a single region are observed.

Table 15 displays the disparate employment effects on regions from changes in project type and the assumed region of construction. In the columns labeled A, the extent of the regional orientation of the projects is shown. Of the five representative project types presented in that table, local flood protection projects show the highest percentage of total labor cost retained in nine of the ten regions. This is reflected in the high median figure of 76 per cent of total labor costs retained in the region in which the project is assumed to be constructed. The corresponding median figure for the other types of projects ranges from 69.5 to 75 per cent of total labor costs retained.

While the variation among project types in the labor cost retained in the region of construction is relatively modest, a rather more substantial variation is shown among the ten regions. Not unexpectedly, Regions II and III demonstrate a substantially higher propensity to retain labor demands than do any of the other regions. The *minimum* percentage of total labor cost retained by these two regions is 78 and 84, respectively. This figure is equaled in only one other case—local flood protection projects assumed to be constructed on the West Coast. While the median percentages of total labor cost retained are 81 and 88 for Regions II and III, the median ranges from 69 per cent to 74 per cent for the other regions.

In the columns labeled B, the range of labor demands imposed on each region from project construction which is assumed to occur in other regions is shown. For any given project type in any region, this range is substantial. Typically, the maximum dollar value is from 30 to 60 per cent greater than the minimum.

Powerhouse construction		Medium concrete dams		Lock and concrete dams		Large multiple-purpose projects		Dredging		Miscellaneous		Median % of gross output retained
A	B	A	B	A	B	A	B	A	B	A	B	
442	60–116	312	30–45	468	35–55	326	28–46	256	36–51	336	27–39	28
953	202–405	602	108–185	834	130–227	599	102–182	473	118–165	586	108–164	54
1,174	374–580	780	225–306	1,053	276–381	724	188–270	532	168–221	810	262–321	66
357	43–74	345	29–55	497	37–67	335	27–46	217	30–39	374	34–54	31
289	36–48	312	28–45	468	32–52	313	23–37	237	31–43	349	30–41	28
289	36–46	288	24–37	454	29–46	300	22–33	251	34–50	336	25–35	27
238	15–22	256	11–20	395	14–24	266	10–16	168	11–14	299	13–18	25
306	44–58	368	38–71	541	54–94	353	40–62	375	103–131	536	106–150	40
255	32–37	267	18–27	410	21–32	274	18–24	187	20–24	324	22–30	26
425	70–114	390	41–73	556	50–89	379	39–66	306	56–75	449	60–87	36
19.5		32		33		32		26		29		

Table 15. Five Representative Project Types in Ten Regions: (A) Total Labor Cost in Each Region of Project Location, and (B) Range of Total Labor Cost Allocated to Region as Project Is Shifted Among Remaining Regions (in dollars per $1,000 of total contract cost)

Region	Large earth fill dams		Local flood protection		Medium concrete dams		Large multiple-purpose projects		Dredging		Median % of total labor cost retained
	A	B	A	B	A	B	A	B	A	B	
I New England	422	7–10	500	6–10	465	8–12	534	8–13	453	11–15	73
II Mid-Atlantic	477	26–38	560	23–39	546	28–49	608	26–49	503	30–42	81
III East North Central	532	66–78	594	44–60	593	58–81	645	49–72	522	42–56	88
IV West North Central	428	7–11	507	6–11	479	7–14	538	6–12	441	7–9	71
V Southeast	422	6–9	507	6–10	472	7–12	533	6–10	447	9–12	72
VI Lower Atlantic	424	5–7	500	5–8	463	6–10	527	6–9	461	10–14	73
VII Kentucky-Tennessee	416	3–4	494	3–5	452	3–5	522	3–4	428	3	69
VIII West South Central	447	12–21	514	8–14	479	7–17	538	7–13	460	15–20	74
IX Mountain	416	4–5	494	4–5	452	4–7	522	4–6	428	4–5	69
X West Coast	441	11–18	527	11–18	492	11–20	552	10–18	460	13–18	74
Median % of total labor cost retained	69.5		76		70.5		75		73		

SUMMARY AND CONCLUSIONS

Proceeding on assumptions regarding the nature of regional preference, we have presented in this chapter some fairly detailed estimates of the regional impact—both industrial and occupational—of the final demands imposed at different geographical points within the nation. Conceptually, the model determines these impacts as a function of (1) the regional preference functions, (2) the intraregional and interregional structure of productive capacity, and (3) the pattern of occupational and industrial demands generated by project construction, as estimated in Chapter II.

In addition to the need for such estimates in our analysis of the social cost of project construction in an unemployed economy, the estimates are important in themselves. Recognizing the degree to which our statistical findings depend upon assumed relationships, we nevertheless can generalize on the regional impact as follows:

1) With the exception of Regions II and III (Mid-Atlantic and East North Central), the industrial demands placed on the region in which the water resource projects are built are primarily in the categories of trade, transportation, and services.

2) A substantial proportion of total industrial demands (more particularly, demands for durable goods) and off-site labor costs accrue to the Mid-Atlantic and East North Central regions, irrespective of the region wherein the water resource project is constructed.

3) Except for Regions II and III, a relatively small percentage of total industrial and off-site labor demands is retained within the region of demand imposition in spite of the local preference shown the region where the project is located in the model.

4) Water projects vary greatly in the demands they create for *local* output and off-site labor demands; while some project types are regionally oriented, others register their demands far from the construction site.

5) While an estimate of the percentage of total labor costs retained in the region of project construction is significant in assessing the local impact of the expenditure, the occupational demands imposed on the project region vary significantly among regions. Likewise, the pattern of occupational demands retained within the region in which the demand is imposed varies significantly among project types.

6) The labor demand for the operatives and kindred workers and the laborers—both of them occupational categories marked by low incomes and high unemployment—which is retained in the region of project construction seldom exceeds 15 per cent to 20 per cent of the total dollar construction cost.

7) As compared to the demands created by the water resource projects,

the gross national product vector typically has the following characteristics: (a) Industrial gross outputs are more heavily distributed
among the nondurable goods manufacturing and service industries
than among durable. (b) Less labor is demanded per dollar of
gross output. (c) Occupational labor demands are more highly
concentrated in the services and farm occupations than in the
craftsmen and operative categories. (d) The orientation is more
regional than that of water projects—except when Regions II and III
are the regions of demand imposition. (e) The nonretained gross
output and labor demands are widely dispersed rather than being
concentrated so heavily in the durable goods supplying regions
(II and III).

SECTORAL DEMANDS, THE PATTERN OF IDLE RESOURCES, AND THE SOCIAL COST OF PUBLIC INVESTMENT

A PROCEDURE FOR ESTIMATING the social cost of public investments when social values diverge from their market counterparts in a less than fully employed economy is presented in this chapter. As is well known, the cost to society of employing additional resources is significantly overstated by factor market prices in such a situation. Indeed, those resources which have no alternative employments cost the society little or nothing if brought into use, even though they are purchased at the market price.[1]

Evaluating the social costs of a public project requires the detailed disaggregation of the input demands generated by the expenditure followed by comparison of these demands with the pattern and degree of unused productive capacity existing in the economy at the time of project construction. Without this detail, the analyst cannot judge the extent to which demanded inputs are supplied from factor stocks that have no simultaneous alternative use. In Chapters II and III, such detailed sectoral demand analyses were presented. Those chapters showed the results when the input demands of twelve types of water resource projects were disaggregated and analyzed in 82-industry and 156-occupation detail. In this chapter, the pattern of unused productive capacity during 1960, roughly representing conditions prevailing in the 1957–64 period, is compared with these detailed input demands to estimate the social cost of project construction.

We proceed as follows: First, the meaning of the opportunity cost of resource use is investigated for the primary factors—labor and capital—under conditions of both full utilization and complete idleness. From this, the kind of cost adjustment required for factor services under con-

---

[1] To claim that the use of unemployed resources is costless is an overstatement. When idle labor is employed the leisure of the unemployed is given up. When idle capital is employed (and partially consumed) the society is foregoing the possibility of an equivalent amount of future capital consumption. Our position in this study rests on the assumption that decreases in leisure of the unemployed come at no disutility within the relevant range. A specific allowance for the value of depreciated capital will be made in the study. For one of the earliest statements of this position, see J. M. Clark, *The Economics of Overhead Costs* (Chicago: University of Chicago Press, 1923), p. 354. Clark makes the point that "under special conditions a public expenditure may be virtually costless to the community, for example, public works used as a means of preventing unemployment. But depreciation is always a cost and should be reckoned with . . . ."

ditions of less than full employment will be apparent. Second, we describe the procedure used to estimate the extent to which input requirements are satisfied by factors which have no alternative employments. At that point, we argue the need for postulating a set of reasonable market-response relationships describing the functioning of the labor and goods markets in order to estimate social costs. Third, a set of expected response functions relating the degree of required cost adjustment to the level of unemployment is explained. These relationships generate a set of factors to convert market costs into opportunity costs for each type of factor input. Finally, these shadow factors are applied to the project inputs developed in Chapters II and III and the reduction in money costs required to approximate opportunity costs for each of the project types is estimated on both a national and a regional basis for the year 1960.

THE MEASUREMENT OF OPPORTUNITY COSTS

Considered most simply, the opportunity cost of any demand imposed on an economy is the value to society of what it foregoes in satisfying the demand. Assume, for example, that an additional ton of steel production is required of the economy. The social cost of this requirement is represented by the alternative output which the resources devoted to steel production (and to the production of the inputs demanded by the steel industry) would have produced were they not used in producing the ton of steel.

Under certain conditions, the value of this alternative output is easily measured. In a competitive and fully employed market economy with long-run equilibrium, the price of labor—the wage rate—will equate the minimum monetary inducement necessary to bring forth the marginal unit of labor with its marginal value product. Likewise, the equilibrium price of capital will equate the minimum inducement necessary to bring forth the next unit of capital with the value of the output which the marginal unit of capital can produce—the marginal value product of capital.[2] This equilibrium price of capital is further defined as the minimum gross return which is just sufficient to cover the initial investment outlay and meet the interest charges. When P_c is the unit price of capital,

$$P_c = c\,(r) + c\,(d) = c\,(r + d)$$

where c is the initial investment cost, r is the rate of return, and d is the rate of depreciation.[3] Thus, in a fully employed economy with com-

[2] The input of labor is defined as the number of man-hours of service by the typical worker. The input of capital is defined as the service of a unit of the existing real plant and equipment with which labor works in producing society's output.
[3] This definition of the cost of capital is fairly standard. See W. E. G. Salter, *Productivity and Technical Change* (Cambridge, England: Cambridge University Press, 1960), pp. 18–20; Dale W. Jorgenson, "Capital Theory and Investment

petitive markets, the social cost of diverted marginal units of labor and capital is measured by their market prices. Assuming no tax or other distortions, the value of the alternative product equals the sum of the payments to the diverted factors.

If we now move from the case of full employment to an economy with unutilized resources, the market price of diverted resources no longer equals opportunity cost.[4] The market solution fails to provide an accurate estimation of the social sacrifice required by factor diversion. To the extent that unemployed labor is hired, society need forego no alternative outputs.[5] Similarly, with idle capital stock the social cost of capital employed in the production of marginal units of output is less than the minimum return necessary to bring forth an additional unit of capital. If the required capital were put to no alternative use, the only cost incurred by society would be the depreciation expense representing capital consumption.[6] This foregone opportunity is measured by $c(d)$ in the above equation.[7] The society, in effect, sacrifices by foregoing the ability to produce in future periods, since the ability would have remained undiminished were the capital left idle.

This brief statement suggests the task involved in estimating the opportunity cost of resource use when unemployment and excess capacity cause money costs to diverge from real costs. First, we must identify the required factors of production. These consist of both the direct factor requirements and the derived demands or second and further rounds of demands. Second, we must numerically define unemployed factors—labor or capital—as a deviation from a target (full employment) level of unemployment by occupation or capacity utilization by industry. Third, we must make reasonable estimates of the alternative use of the required units of labor and capital—are these factor units drawn from the pool of the unemployed or are they drawn from alternative employments? Finally, we must assign to each unit of each factor the value of the social loss incurred by its diversion.

Behavior," *American Economic Review, Papers and Proceedings*, Vol. 53 (May 1963), pp. 247–59; and Bert G. Hickman, *Investment Demand and U.S. Economic Growth* (Washington: Brookings Institution, 1965), pp. 29 and 60.

[4] Implicit in this shift from the fully employed economy to the economy with less than full employment is the assumption of price inflexibility. Were prices completely flexible, the case with less than full employment would be but a transitory phenomenon. For convenience, we assume that the market price of the employed factors is equal to the value of their marginal products even though some of the factors are less than fully employed.

[5] See footnote 1, Chapter IV.

[6] Society has already foregone the rate of return on the capital by permitting it to lie idle.

[7] Implicit is the assumption that depreciation results only from wear and tear on the physical capital. Because of obsolescence, charging the entire depreciation cost to the social cost of using the otherwise idle capital may result in some overestimation of social opportunity cost.

THE NATURE OF THE SHADOW ADJUSTMENT

In Chapters II and III, the total demand imposed on the economy by water project construction was disaggregated into its value-added components—employee compensation, corporate profits, net interest, indirect business taxes, capital consumption allowances (depreciation), proprietor and rental income, and imports. The sum of these (plus the amount of unallocated costs) for any project equaled the value of the total construction contract expenditure. In a fully employed economy, each of these components (and, hence, the total contract expenditure) represents a true social cost. Defense of this statement will clarify the form of shadow adjustment made in our analysis.

Without question, employee compensation and proprietor and rental income, as estimates of direct factor payments, reflect the opportunity returns foregone at the margin by society in diverting fully employed factors of production.[8] The money costs of these factors represent the value of the marginal output which they would be producing in alternative employments and, hence, reflect the social sacrifice required in their diversion. By similar reasoning, dollar estimates of capital consumption, net interest, and corporate profits also reflect foregone opportunity returns.[9] Were the diverted units of capital not required, they would be utilized in the most desirable alternative production process where their price would reflect social value.

To justify as social costs the dollar estimates of the indirect business tax components of value added is substantially more difficult. However, the practice is consistent with the position of Simon Kuznets that government can be treated in social accounting as a business.[10] With this interpretation, business taxes represent government revenue earned from services "sold" to business firms, and this revenue is used to cover the labor and capital costs of government operation. In full employment, the diversion of these units of labor and capital to government use represents a reduction of alternative outputs of social value and, hence, the imposition of opportunity cost.[11]

---

[8] It is well recognized that the definition of these categories is largely institutionally determined. As such, the dollar estimates in each category fail to reflect accurately the relative payments to the theoretical factors of production. For example, a part of the payments to labor is captured in the category of proprietor and rental income rather than in the category of employee compensation. See Richard and Nancy Ruggles, *National Income Accounts and Income Analysis* (New York: McGraw-Hill, 1956), pp. 125–26. Notwithstanding this lack of conformity, these estimates are the sole statistical indication of the relative functional breakdown, and it is on this basis that their use here is defended.

[9] Dollar estimates of capital consumption embody a unique set of statistical problems causing their estimation to be highly problematical. See Ruggles and Ruggles, *ibid.*, p. 114.

[10] Simon Kuznets, *National Income and Its Composition, 1919–1938*, Vol. 1 (New York: National Bureau of Economic Research, 1941), pp. 31–34.

[11] Earl Rolph, it should be noted, has a substantially different view of the proper

That part of project construction cost devoted to the purchase of imported goods also represents social cost in a fully employed economy. Assuming the necessity for a nation to maintain a long-run balance of trade, sufficient resources to earn the foreign exchange to pay for the required imports must be diverted to the production of exports. Such diversion again implies a reduction of socially valuable alternative outputs and, hence, opportunity costs.

On these bases, then, each of the components of value added and, therefore, the total value added (or total project cost) represents social cost in a fully employed economy. Relying on this rationale, we can now state the appropriate adjustment of money costs in an economy which is less than fully employed. In the case of the direct factor payments— employee compensation, net interest, and corporate profits—we adjust money costs by use of a set of synthetic response functions relating the probability that a given increment in the demand for labor and capital will be drawn from otherwise unemployed resources to the level of occupational unemployment and excess industrial capacity. The capital consumption component, representing a reduction in the economy's ability to produce in the future, is accepted as an approximation of real cost, even if the capital represented were otherwise unemployed. Because of the practical impossibility of tracing the detailed pattern of resource use required by expenditures for the remaining value-added components —proprietor and rental income, indirect business taxes, imports, and unallocated costs—their sum is adjusted in the same direction and to the same extent that the sum of the employee compensation, net interest, corporate profits, and depreciation components is adjusted.[12] Implicit in

treatment of indirect taxes. He concludes that indirect taxes are properly treated as "income generated by the resources in the economy" but diverted to the government. See Rolph, *The Theory of Fiscal Economics* (Berkeley: University of California Press, 1956), p. 69. Under both the Rolph and Kuznets definitions, however, indirect business taxes represent opportunity costs—the value of alternatives foregone.

[12] In order more accurately to adjust these components in periods of less than full employment, the following information on the pattern of resource use would be essential: For the proprietor and rental income component, we would have to separate the rent and proprietor income, determine the occupational breakdown for those single proprietors earning income from the exogenous claim, ascertain the proportions of their income which is payment for labor services and the proportion which accrues to their capital, and estimate the value of the alternative use of their labor and capital services. For the rental income component, we would have to determine the nature of the land resource drawn into use by the exogenous demand and estimate the value of its alternative use. For the indirect business tax, two alternatives are possible. If we adopt the Kuznets formulation, the structure of governmental services rendered in the production for the exogenous claim would have to be determined, the value of the labor and capital inputs in an alternative use estimated, and the value of the public depreciation component ascertained. If we adopt the Rolph formulation, we would have to divide the indirect business tax by industry into its labor and capital components, and then evaluate these components as the existing labor and capital components in

this procedure is the assumption that the pattern of factor demands imposed by the sum of these remaining expenditures is the same as the pattern imposed by the traceable factor demands.

EXPECTED LABOR AND CAPITAL
RESPONSE FUNCTIONS

To adjust money costs for deviations from a fully employed economy, we use a set of expected relationships incorporating a judgment concerning the response of labor and capital goods markets to increments in demand under varying conditions of unemployment. Assuming a labor force which is occupationally immobile, these functions specify an inverse relationship between the level of resource utilization and the extent to which incremental demands are satisfied from otherwise unutilized stocks. The general shape of these relationships is established by reference to the two extreme cases embodying clearly unrealistic states of the world.

In the first of these extreme cases, any increment to factor demand is satisfied from the pool of unemployed factors whenever the economy deviates from full employment. Either by the direct satisfaction of the demand increment through the employment of an idle factor unit, or by the indirect establishment of the linkage from the increment in demand to the pool of the unemployed, this case requires that the bumping process insure a decrease in unemployment equivalent to the increment of demand.

At the opposite extreme, incremental factor demands are supplied entirely by the diversion of factors from alternative employments, even though unemployed factors exist. Such diversion suggests a contraction in the quantity or quality (or both) of alternative productive activities with the social loss equal to the value of the output foregone. Market factor costs are equivalent to this social loss.

To be sure, such realities as institutional restraints, limited geographic mobility, construction company practice of importing its skilled labor force, and substantial inadequacies in the quantity and quality of labor market information strongly suggest that the first extreme response is achieved with little regularity. That all incremental factor demands should be supplied by diversion from alternative employments is equally unrealistic in an unemployed economy. On this basis, the behavior of

---

that industry were evaluated. For the import component, we would need to estimate the labor and capital inputs to the export commodities earning the foreign exchange required to purchase the imports, and then estimate the value of these labor and capital inputs in an alternative use. For unallocated costs, the labor and capital demands represented by these costs would have to be ascertained and their value in an alternative use estimated. As stated in the text, we have no empirical basis for tracing the structural composition of these labor and capital inputs.

the factor markets, in the following analysis, is assumed to be intermediate to these extremes.

Accepting the likelihood of such an intermediate response pattern in the real world and presuming short-run occupational immobility, we postulate that the extent to which an increment to labor demand is satisfied by the employment of otherwise idle units of labor is positively related to the level of occupational unemployment. The higher the rate of unemployment, the greater the expectation (1) that an otherwise idle worker will appear at the hiring window when the incremental job is being filled, and (2) that employers requiring additional labor will hire from the pool of unemployed rather than decrease their output or work their existing labor force overtime. This area has not been studied in the depth necessary for the establishment of empirically specified response functions relating the rate of unemployment and the probability of satisfying the increment in demand with a unit of unemployed labor. Nevertheless, it is this type of relationship which we use in estimating shadow labor cost.

A similarly pragmatic approach is adopted to the estimation of the response of supply to increments of demand for existing capital services. Again it is assumed that the response of industry to increments of demand depends on the level of excess industrial capacity; that demand increments are far less likely to displace existing production when substantial excess capacity exists than when production is at capacity output. In this case, also, insufficient study has been undertaken to permit empirically specified relationships. Despite this deficiency, reasonable cases are postulated and applied in estimating the relationship of the social to the financial costs of capital employment.

In Figures 7 and 8, synthetic functions are pictured in which the percentage of incremental labor and capital demands which will be supplied from unutilized resources are related to the level of unemployment and idle capacity. For each of the major occupational categories and for capital, two boundary response functions and an intermediate function have been used to secure estimates of the percentage of labor and capital drawn from the idle pool. In Figure 7 showing labor response, the family of upper- and lower-bound functions (one function for each major occupational category) lies within the H and L functions, respectively. The family of intermediate or "best-estimate" (I) labor functions falls within the shaded area. In Figure 8 showing capital response functions, the upper-bound (H) and lower-bound (L) functions are shown in addition to the function taken as the best estimate.

On the abscissa of each of these figures we have plotted the rate of unemployment or idle capacity, r, existing at a point in time in any occupation (Figure 7) or industry (Figure 8). The ordinate measures the proportion of the increment to the demand for a factor which will be supplied from the stock of unutilized factor services, p. In both

FIGURE 7. LABOR RESPONSE FUNCTIONS

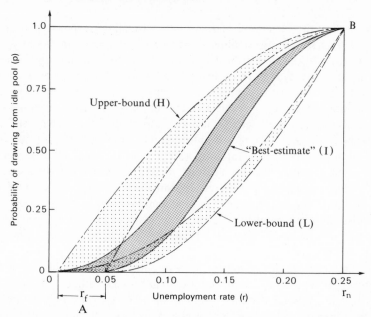

diagrams, the points labeled r_f are taken to be the rate of unemployment for any occupation (or industry) which represents the "full employment" of that occupation (or industry). In the case of the labor functions, r_f is defined by the national unemployment rate experienced by each occupational group in 1953. That year, in our judgment, represents a year of minimum unemployment without undue inflationary stresses.[13] For

---

[13] In 1953, national unemployment was 2.5 per cent of the civilian labor force. The unemployment rates for the major occupational categories in 1953 were as follows:

Category	Percent
Professional, technical, & kindred workers	0.9
Managers, officials, & proprietors	0.9
Clerical & kindred workers	1.7
Sales workers	2.1
Craftsmen, foremen, & kindred workers	2.6
Operatives & kindred workers	3.2
Service workers	3.6
Farmers and farm workers	1.0
Laborers, except farm and mine	6.1

See U.S. Department of Labor, *Manpower Report of the President* and *A Report on Manpower Requirements, Resources, Utilization, and Training*, Washington, 1966, p. 170. With the exception of the category for laborers, except farm and mine, these unemployment rates were taken as definitions of full employment for their respective occupational categories. For laborers except farm and mine, 5 per cent was taken to define full employment. Because of well-known reporting problems for transient laborers, 6.1 per cent was felt to be an overstatement of the effective level of unemployment in this category when it is fully employed.

FIGURE 8. CAPITAL RESPONSE FUNCTIONS

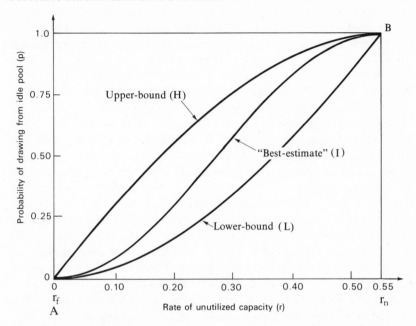

the capital functions, full capacity utilization is assumed to occur when the rate of excess capacity is zero.[14]

The points labeled r_n on the diagrams signify the rate of unemployment or excess capacity at which an increment to factor demand would be entirely supplied from otherwise unutilized resources. In the case of the labor response functions, r_n is taken to be .25. For the capital functions, the rate is .55. These numbers are the estimated rates of unemployment and unutilized capacity at the height of the depression of the thirties.[15] In choosing these figures, it is assumed that under such conditions all would agree that increments to the demand for labor and capital are satisfied with no displacement of alternative outputs.

In Figure 7, the intermediate family of functions (I) representing the best estimate are sine functions describing a not unlikely response

---

[14] This is not necessarily equal to 100 per cent of theoretical capacity; see Appendix 8 for the meaning of the term "excess capacity" as it is used in this analysis. Appendix 8 also describes the process of estimating industrial capacity utilization employed in this study.

[15] In 1933, 24.9 per cent of the civilian labor force was classified as unemployed. See U.S. Council of Economic Advisers, *1964 Supplement to Economic Indicators*, Washington, 1964. Donald C. Streever has estimated the percentage of national productive capacity utilized at the height of the Depression to be between 42 per cent and 45 per cent. See Streever, *Capacity Utilization and Business Investment* (Urbana: University of Illinois, Bureau of Economic and Business Research, 1960), pp. 40 and 64.

of the labor market to increments in demand.[16] These best-estimate labor functions increase slowly as the observed rate of unemployment begins to exceed the full employment level; then, as unemployment rates enter the 8 per cent to 15 per cent range, the percentage of labor drawn from the idle pool increases rapidly. When unemployment rates reach 18 per cent to 20 per cent, nearly all of the labor demanded is drawn from the idle pool and increments to the rate of unemployment induce the very small increments in the estimated idle percentage.

This response pattern is judged to be an accurate portrayal of actual labor market experience. Thus, as the economy moves away from full employment (2.5 per cent) and into the 4 per cent to 5 per cent range, labor markets continue to experience the same kinds of pressures as with less unemployment, but admittedly with less force. Similarly, the upper end of the best-estimate function is consistent with experience. Even though nearly all demands are met by unemployed resources, certain skills remain in short supply and demands for them can only be met by diversion from other activities.[17] The upper-bound and lower-bound functions will be treated as practical limits within which p will fall for any observed occupational unemployment rate.

In Figure 8, much the same sort of response relationships are posited for capital. Again, the upper-bound and lower-bound and the intermediate best-estimate functions are drawn between points A and B. As in the case of labor, the boundary functions are treated as circumscribing the behavioral response pattern of the operators of capital facilities to increments in the demand for capital. The shape of the best-estimate function is explained by reasoning analogous to that employed for the best-estimate labor functions.

The required opportunity cost factors are derived directly from these labor and capital response functions. For any rate of unemployment (or excess capacity), the intermediate market response relationships are assumed to provide the best estimate of the proportion of any demand increment which will be supplied from otherwise unutilized resources and, therefore, resources with no opportunity costs. Conversely, they are also assumed to provide the best estimate of the proportion of the increment requiring factor diversion and, hence, imposing social cost. While the proportion supplied from the stock of unutilized factors is p, the proportion of the increment entailing lost social opportunities is $(1 - p)$. On this basis, we assume that the opportunity cost of factor inputs of a particular occupation or industry is equal to $(1 - p)$ times

[16] The mathematical statement of the functions employed for each occupational category, both for the upper-bound and lower-bound functions and for the intermediate or best-estimate functions, are given in Appendix 9.

[17] These relationships were derived by assuming that the percentage (p) is an appropriate function of the sine of the deviation of the unemployment rate from full employment. By requiring the functions to pass through both the full employment point and the unit probability point, the parameters are immediately derived.

the estimated market or money cost of these demands.[18] In our further analysis, these $(1 - p)$ values are referred to as shadow (labor and capital) factors and applied to the detailed occupational and industrial demands of water resource construction estimated in Chapters II and III.

THE OPPORTUNITY COST OF PUBLIC INVESTMENT: 1957–64

In estimating the opportunity costs for construction of water resource projects, we apply the synthetic response functions to the detailed data on the level of idle resources as a means of deriving shadow labor factors (by occupation) and shadow capital factors (by industry) for the year 1960. As already stated, this year is roughly representative of the years 1957–64. First, we assume that project construction draws factors from national markets for labor and goods. In this case, data on *national* occupational unemployment and excess industrial capacity are utilized in deriving the shadow labor and capital factors. These factors are then applied to the detailed estimates of labor and capital demands by project type, as determined in Chapter II, so as to yield an estimate of real costs as a percentage of money cost. Second, we assume that each of the project types are constructed in each of the ten regions, with labor and other resource demands distributed among the regions as determined in Chapter III. In this case, regional unemployment rates by occupational categories provide the basis for deriving the shadow labor factors. Real costs depend upon the geographical location of project construction and the unemployment pattern in each region. (Appendix 9 presents the mathematical formulation of the models of social cost estimation implemented here.)

A National Analysis

In the national analysis, unemployment rates were computed for the 156 detailed occupations from the 1960 Census of Population.[19] For each occupation, the number of employed persons is compared with the number of persons in the experienced civilian labor force to provide the estimated occupational unemployment rate. These rates ranged from less than .25 per cent for a few detailed occupations in the category

[18] As Stephen A. Marglin has put it: "[The] appropriate shadow wage rate is the marginal opportunity cost of the force actually drawn from alternative employments [the market wage rate] multiplied by the percentage which this force forms of the total labor employed in this category in system construction." Marglin, "Objectives of Water-Resource Development: A General Statement," in Arthur Maass *et al.*, *Design of Water Resource Systems* (Cambridge: Harvard University Press, 1962), p. 51.
[19] U.S. Department of Commerce, Bureau of the Census, "Occupational Characteristics," *U.S. Census of Population: 1960*, Final Report PC(2)–7A, Washington, 1963, data from Tables 1 and 2.

for professional, technical, and kindred workers to over 20 per cent in some of the detailed occupations in the category of craftsmen, foremen, and kindred workers. Estimates of the rates of excess capacity by industry in 1960 were an average of capacity utilization estimates drawn from a number of sources. (Appendix 8 describes in detail the estimation procedure adopted in securing rates of excess industrial capacity.)

Table 16 presents the results of applying the shadow labor factors obtained from the intermediate best-estimate functions to the occupational breakdown of total labor costs. For each project type, the shadow labor cost is presented as a percentage of total dollar cost by major occupational categories. Presuming the intermediate response functions to be accurate descriptions of labor market behavior, the estimated social costs for labor among project types range from 80.8 per cent to 91.3 per cent of the money labor costs. Using the more conservative lower-bound response functions yields social labor cost estimates among project types which range from 88.0 per cent to 95.3 per cent of their financial counterparts. Application of the upper-bound labor functions yields estimates which range from 66.6 to 78.4 per cent of money labor costs. Given the rather disparate pattern of occupational demands among the project types, this variation within each set of response functions is not unexpected. For example, dredging projects impose large demands on sailors and deck hands—a high unemployment occupation. As a result, the social cost of labor used for dredging ranges from 66.6 per cent (upper-bound functions) to 88.0 per cent (lower-bound functions) of financial labor costs. The intermediate functions yield a percentage estimate of 80.8. On the other hand, because powerhouse construction imposes heavy demands on the more fully employed skilled occupations, estimates of the social cost of labor use for such projects range from

Table 16. Best Estimate of Shadow Labor Cost as a Percentage of Total Labor Cost by Project Type and Occupation, and Related Data

Item	Large earth fill dams	Small earth fill dams	Local flood protection	Pile dikes
Professional, technical, & kindred workers	99.6%	99.5%	99.5%	99.4%
Managers, officials, & proprietors	99.7	99.7	99.6	99.5
Clerical & kindred workers	98.6	98.7	98.6	98.6
Sales workers	99.2	99.2	99.2	99.2
Craftsmen, foremen, & kindred workers	85.7	79.3	77.9	83.3
Operatives & kindred workers	90.5	87.4	89.9	78.6
Service workers	97.9	97.9	97.9	98.0
Laborers, except farm & mine	72.9	72.9	72.9	72.9
Farmers & farm workers	100.0	100.0	100.0	100.0
Shadow labor cost as percentage of total labor cost	90.0%	86.3%	84.9%	85.6%
Total shadow labor cost[a]	$551	$572	$567	$513
Total money labor cost[a]	612	662	667	600
Weighted average unemployment rate[b]	5.85	6.62	7.15	6.78

[a] Data in dollars per $1,000 of contract cost.
[b] The weights used in computing this average were the dollars of money labor cost in each occupation.

78.4 per cent (upper-bound functions) to 95.3 per cent (lower-bound functions) of money costs. The best estimate is 91.3 per cent.

The range of adjustment required among the occupational groups substantially exceeds that required among project types. While for some occupations opportunity costs equal money costs, the social cost of employing unskilled laborers is estimated to be less than 75 per cent of the money cost.

Of further interest is the variation in the extent of the adjustment required within a single major occupational category among the project types. Because of the differing composition of the detailed occupational demands within, say, the category of craftsmen, foremen, and kindred workers, the best estimate ranges from 77.9 per cent for local flood protection to 93.4 per cent for dredging. For the operatives and kindred workers, the range of the best estimate is from 61.4 per cent to 90.7 per cent. It is precisely this sort of distribution that the detailed procedure adopted in this analysis is able to isolate.

In the last row of Table 16, a weighted average unemployment rate is displayed for each type of project. Computed from occupational unemployment rates weighted by dollars of labor cost, these rates can be interpreted as the rate of unemployment existing in the "labor force" in which the typical dollar of labor cost is spent in each project type. In general, these weighted averages vary inversely with the opportunity cost estimates. It is noteworthy that in every project type the weighted average unemployment rate exceeds the national censal unemployment rate of 4.93. Moreover, the typical dollar spent for any of the water resource project types has a greater unemployment reduction potential than the typical dollar spent for the bundle of goods comprising the gross national product. This is reinforced by the estimate that in all

Levees	Revetments	Power-house construction	Medium concrete dams	Lock & concrete dams	Large multiple-purpose projects	Dredging	Miscellaneous	Range
99.6%	99.4%	99.5%	99.6%	99.5%	99.6%	99.6%	99.6%	99.4–99.6%
99.6	99.1	99.7	99.7	99.0	99.7	82.9	99.7	82.9–99.7
98.6	98.6	98.7	98.6	98.6	98.6	98.6	98.6	98.6–98.7
99.2	99.2	99.2	99.2	99.2	99.2	99.2	99.2	99.2
83.4	89.3	86.7	85.2	85.6	85.5	93.4	84.5	77.9–93.4
82.1	74.0	88.8	88.4	88.5	88.8	61.4	90.7	61.4–90.7
98.0	98.0	97.9	98.0	98.0	97.9	97.6	97.9	97.9–98.0
72.9	72.9	72.9	72.9	72.9	72.9	72.9	72.9	72.9
100.0	100.0	100.0	100.0	100.0	100.0	100.0	100.0	100.0
86.4%	85.8%	91.3%	88.6%	89.5%	88.3%	80.8%	90.0%	80.8–91.3%
$498	$444	$631	$597	$613	$635	$502	$544	
577	517	691	674	685	719	621	605	
6.59	6.69	5.44	6.25	5.99	6.22	7.62	5.89	5.44–7.62

Table 17. Total Money Capital Cost and Best Estimate of Shadow Capital Cost for the Large Multiple-Purpose Project (in dollars per $1,000 of total contract cost)

Industrial category	Capital cost		Shadow as % of money capital cost
	Total money[a]	Total shadow	
Agriculture, forestry, & fisheries	.77	.72	93
Mining, including crude petroleum	8.68	8.32	96
Nondurable goods manufacturing	11.43	11.01	96
Durable goods manufacturing	49.78	43.11	87
Lumber & wood products	.67	.64	96
Stone, clay, & glass products	11.43	9.76	85
Primary metals	11.16	9.29	83
Fabricated metals	6.69	6.36	95
Nonelectrical machinery, except construction	6.84	5.86	86
Construction machinery	4.79	4.09	85
Electrical machinery	5.96	5.17	87
Transportation equipment	1.32	1.05	79
Miscellaneous	.91	.89	98
Transportation & warehousing	8.40	8.14	97
Wholesale & retail trade	8.47	8.46	99
Services	24.43	24.03	98
Total	111.96	103.79	93

[a] The sum of the values of capital consumption allowance, net interest, and corporate profits.

cases except one the labor demand generated by the water resource projects exceeds that generated by the GNP vector (see Table 7).

In Tables 17 and 18, a similar shadow pricing analysis is shown for the money capital costs generated by water project construction.[20] In Table 17, a detailed industry breakdown is presented for the large multiple-purpose project. In this case, the rates of industrial excess capacity serve the same function as the rates of occupational unemployment served in the analysis of shadow labor costs. The social cost of the capital required for constructing the multiple-purpose project is estimated in the table to be 93 per cent of the money cost using the intermediate response function. Application of the upper-bound and lower-bound response functions yields estimates of 83 per cent and 95 per cent, respectively. Like the variations among occupations, the shadow percentages vary substantially among industries. For example, while the best estimate is 99 per cent for wholesale and retail trade, it is but 79 per cent for transportation equipment.

[20] As will be recalled, we have estimated the total capital costs of project construction to be the sum of net interest, depreciation expense, and corporate profits generated by the bill of final demands. These money cost estimates were presented in Table 7 for the twelve project types. The interest and profit components of capital cost are adjusted in the analysis of social cost. The estimates of depreciation expense, representing reduction of the ability to produce in the future, are maintained intact.

Table 18. Total Money Capital Cost and Best Estimate of Shadow Capital Cost for the Twelve Project Types (in dollars per $1,000 of total contract costs)

Project type	Capital cost		Shadow as % of money capital cost
	Total money[a]	Total shadow	
Large earth fill dams	119	111	94
Small earth fill dams	135	126	94
Local flood protection	109	103	94
Pile dikes	114	108	95
Levees	93	88	95
Revetments	157	151	96
Powerhouse construction	172	156	91
Medium concrete dams	121	111	92
Lock and concrete dams	159	147	92
Large multiple-purpose projects	112	104	93
Dredging	99	90	91
Miscellaneous	137	128	94

[a] The sum of the values of capital consumption allowance, net interest, and corporate profits.

Again, the additional information gained by working with the detailed sectoral definitions is seen. Within the aggregated durable goods manufacturing category, the detailed industry percentages range from 79 (transportation equipment) to 98 (miscellaneous manufacturing).

Table 18 summarizes the results obtained by applying the capital shadow factors derived from the intermediate best-estimate response function to detailed industrial capital cost data for all of the project types. As with the application of shadow estimates to labor inputs, there is substantial variation among the project types. The best estimate of the opportunity cost of the capital used ranges from 91 per cent (both powerhouse construction and dredging) to 96 per cent (revetments) of the money cost. With the upper-bound function, the social cost of the capital used ranges from 79 per cent of stated cost for powerhouse construction to 90 per cent of stated cost for the construction of revetments. The range of estimates obtained from the lower-bound functions is from 95 per cent (dredging) to 98 per cent (revetments).

In Table 19, the adjustment to total contract cost required by the upper-bound and lower-bound response functions and the best-estimate functions is shown. As discussed earlier, the adjustment to total contract costs is obtained by applying to the project costs which cannot be classified as labor or capital costs (unallocated costs, indirect business taxes, proprietor and rental income, and imports), the combined ratio of shadow labor plus shadow capital costs to the sum of money labor and money capital costs for that project type.[21] This procedure assumes

[21] For example, applying the intermediate response relationship, real labor costs for the large multiple-purpose project were estimated to be $635 and real capital costs to be $104 for a total of $739 of real costs. This compares with $719 of

Table 19. Shadow Cost for the Twelve Project Types by Upper-Bound, Lower-Bound, and Best-Estimate Functions (in dollars per $1,000 of total contract cost)

Project type	Lower bound	Best estimate	Upper bound
Large earth fill dams	781	906	949
Small earth fill dams	740	876	932
Local flood protection	715	860	924
Pile dikes	742	870	925
Levees	749	876	929
Revetments	765	883	932
Powerhouse construction	786	913	953
Medium concrete dams	756	891	941
Lock and concrete dams	770	900	946
Large multiple-purpose projects	757	889	940
Dredging	687	822	889
Miscellaneous	780	906	949

that the pattern of resource demands generated by these remaining costs is identical to the pattern generated by the labor and capital demands which were traced. As seen in Table 19, the estimates of social cost again vary significantly among project types. Adopting the lower-bound and upper-bound response functions, the opportunity costs per $1,000 of money costs among project types range from $687 to $786 and $889 to $953, respectively. With the intermediate or best-estimate relationships, the range is from $822 to $913. Of particular interest are the dredging and local flood protection projects. While the intermediate cost estimates for the project types are typically well above $875, dredging displays a social cost estimate of but $822 and local flood protection projects a social cost of $860.

On a national basis for the 1957–64 period, it is reasonable to claim that the money costs of project construction do not provide an accurate estimate of the opportunities sacrificed by the society. Because of the widespread unemployment of labor and capital, resources could have been devoted to public investment with less social cost than money cost estimates would indicate. For the national pattern of unused labor and capital in 1960, we would, on the basis of the two boundary response functions, claim that real costs account for but 70 per cent to 95 per cent of the market value of water project construction, depending on the type under consideration. On the basis of this estimate, it appears that a reduction of 5 per cent to 30 per cent of the 1960 costs of water resource construction, depending on project type and response function, would provide substantially more accurate estimates of the opportunity costs of resource use.

money labor costs and $112 of money capital costs, or a total of $831 of money costs. The resulting ratio of total real labor and capital to total money labor and capital costs of .889 is then applied to the $169 of remaining costs. Of the total $1,000 of contract cost, the best estimate claims $889 to be true social costs.

A Regional Analysis

The real costs of project construction are estimated in this section for each project type as the location of the construction site is shifted among regions. For this study, we adjusted the regional resource demands estimated in Chapter III for regional patterns of unemployment. But because regional estimates of industrial excess capacity were not available, the shadow capital factors utilized in the national analysis are also employed in the regional analysis.[22]

In adjusting the labor costs, however, a substantially more complicated procedure is adopted. First, one state in each of the regions is designated as the site of project construction when the project is assumed to be constructed in that region.[23] All of the on-site labor costs are assigned to the state containing the project site, and these money costs are adjusted by shadow labor factors derived from the synthetic labor response functions and the detailed occupational unemployment rates in that state.[24] Off-site labor demands for project construction assumed to occur in any region were allocated among all of the regions according to the regional allocation rules discussed in Chapter III. These demands are assumed to be met from within the region to which they are allocated and, consequently, the money costs represented by these demands are adjusted by shadow labor factors estimated from the labor response functions and the detailed occupational unemployment rates within each of the regions.[25] Again the adjustment to total contract cost is obtained by applying the ratio of the sum of shadow labor and capital costs and the sum of money labor and money capital costs to the remaining cost of any project type.[26]

In Tables 20 and 21, the results of this adjustment procedure are summarized for five representative project types. A few rather striking aspects of the data stand out. While substantial differences in the size of the cost adjustment have been observed among project types, Tables 20 and 21 isolate the differences in cost adjustment for a single project type as its geographic location is shifted. Without question, the cost variation resulting from the change in location of a single project type greatly exceeds the variation among project types constructed in the same region. In the national analysis, the range of cost adjustment among project types is less than 10 percentage points for any of the response functions adopted (Table 19). But in all cases, the range is 15 or

[22] See Appendix 8 for details of the procedure.
[23] These states are Massachusetts, Pennsylvania, Indiana, Iowa, Georgia, West Virginia, Kentucky, Texas, Colorado, and California, for Regions I through X, respectively.
[24] These unemployment rates were calculated from the U.S. Department of Commerce, Bureau of the Census, "Detailed Characteristics" (by state), *U.S. Census of Population, 1960*, Washington, 1963.
[25] *Ibid.*
[26] See footnote 21, Chapter IV.

Table 20. Best Estimate of (A) Shadow Labor Cost as a Percentage of Total Labor Cost, and (B) Weighted Average Unemployment Rates[b] for Five Representative Project Types in Ten Regions of Project Location, with Related Data

Region	Large earth fill dams		Local flood protection		Medium concrete dams		Large multiple-purpose projects		Dredging	
	A	B	A	B	A	B	A	B	A	B
I New England	88%	5.6	82%	7.3	88%	6.2	87%	6.4	83%	6.9
II Mid-Atlantic	80	6.9	74	8.7	82	7.2	81	7.3	76	8.3
IIi East North Central	90	5.0	89	5.9	92	5.3	92	5.2	89	5.6
IV West North Central	87	5.3	84	6.9	89	5.6	89	5.5	88	5.9
V Southeast	93	4.3	92	5.2	94	4.8	94	4.8	88	5.8
VI Lower Atlantic	75	7.9	65	10.4	74	8.7	73	8.8	73	9.0
VII Kentucky-Tennessee	81	6.8	75	8.5	81	7.5	80	7.7	77	8.4
VIII West South Central	92	4.6	91	5.5	93	5.2	93	5.1	86	6.2
IX Mountain	91	4.7	92	5.5	93	5.1	93	5.0	94	3.7
X West Coast	85	6.3	82	7.6	86	6.8	86	6.6	74	9.0
Range of percentages	75–93		65–92		74–94		73–94		73–94	
Median percentage	87.5		83		88		88		84.5	
Total money labor cost[a]	$612		$667		$674		$719		$621	
Total shadow labor cost[a]	551		567		597		635		502	
Shadow labor cost as percentage of total labor cost	90		85		89		88		81	

[a] Data in dollars per $1,000 of contract cost.
[b] The weights used in computing these averages were the dollars of money labor costs in each type of project and region.

more percentage points when the construction of a single project type is shifted among geographic regions (Table 21). Indeed, in the case of local flood protection projects, the range exceeds 24 percentage points—a substantial influence on cost adjustment attributable to geographic location. When labor costs alone are considered (Table 20), the variation of the proportion of social to money costs due to project location is 18 or more percentage points for all project categories—with a range for flood protection of 27 percentage points.

The influence of geographic unemployment is most clearly seen by comparing the cost adjustments required by project construction located in the Lower Atlantic region which is characterized by high unemployment with the adjustments required by project construction in other regions. As Table 20 shows, for all five project types the labor cost adjustment required for projects constructed in the Lower Atlantic region is at least 11 percentage points greater than the *median* cost adjustment required for the ten regions and from 18 to 27 percentage points in excess of the minimum required cost adjustment (for that project type and the best-estimate response functions). Similar cost adjustment comparisons exist when total contract costs are considered. For example, Table 21 shows real project costs for the medium concrete dams to be but 77 per cent of money costs when the intermediate response functions are applied and the project is constructed in the Lower Atlantic region. But *median* regional social costs are 89 per cent of money costs, and the social costs for project construction in the Southeast (Region V) are 94 per cent of money costs.

Because of the rather unusual pattern of resource demands (especially labor) imposed by dredging and local flood protection projects, both the level and geographical pattern of cost adjustment differ substantially from the other project types. As the national analysis in Table 19 reveals, the cost adjustment required for these two project types substantially exceeds that required for the other projects irrespective of response function. In all regions save two, the cost adjustment required for these project types exceeds the adjustment for the other types shown. The two exceptions shown in Table 21 are dredging projects in the West North Central region (IV) and in the Mountain region (IX). The significant differences are caused by the unique occupational labor requirements imposed by dredging projects. While, for example, the smallest cost adjustment required for dredging projects occurs when they are constructed in Regions III and IX, the smallest cost adjustment required for all of the remaining project types is associated with construction in the Southeast region (V).

Many of the same patterns may be observed by studying the weighted average unemployment rates by project type and region displayed in Table 20. As in the national analysis, these rates signify the level of unemployment existing in the labor force from which each project type

Table 21. Best Estimate of Shadow Cost as a Percentage of Total Contract Cost for Five Representative Project Types in Ten Regions of Project Location

	Region	Large earth fill dams	Local flood protection	Medium concrete dams	Large multiple-purpose projects	Dredging	Range of percentages	Median percentage
I	New England	89	84	88	87	84	84–89	86.5
II	Mid-Atlantic	82	77	84	82	78	77–84	80.5
III	East North Central	91	90	92	92	90	90–92	91.0
IV	West North Central	88	85	90	89	89	85–90	87.5
V	Southeast	93	93	94	94	88	88–94	91.5
VI	Lower Atlantic	78	69	77	76	75	69–78	73.5
VII	Kentucky-Tennessee	83	78	83	81	79	78–83	80.5
VIII	West South Central	92	92	93	93	87	87–93	90.0
IX	Mountain	92	92	93	93	94	92–94	93.0
X	West Coast	86	84	87	87	76	76–87	81.5
	Range of percentages	78–93	69–93	77–94	76–94	75–94		
	Median percentage	88.5	84.5	89	88	85.5		

secures its labor as project construction is shifted among regions. The greater the weighted average unemployment rate, the greater the unemployment-reducing potential of the expenditure. It is interesting that of the fifty rates displayed in Table 20, only six are less than or equal to the national unemployment rate of 4.93 per cent for the time period under consideration. Three of these six rates occur when the project type is the large earth fill dam, and all of them are included in the Southeast (V), West South Central (VIII), or Mountain (IX) regions. More important, no less than sixteen of the fifty examples have weighted unemployment rates in excess of 7.0 per cent, and local flood protection in the Lower Atlantic region displays a rate of 10.4 per cent—over twice the national unemployment rate. The unemployment-reducing potential of this type of project constructed in that location is significantly higher than the unemployment-reducing potential of an equivalent amount spent on the basket of goods comprising the gross national product.

SUMMARY AND CONCLUSIONS

The possibilities of adjusting the money costs of public investments to allow for the use of otherwise unemployed labor and capital resources have been explored in this chapter. First, the logic of such adjustment was developed and the need to establish reasonable market response functions explained. Next, a set of synthetic response functions was assumed to be best estimates of, and to bound the range of, the operation of real markets. On the basis of these functions, shadow labor and capital factors for unemployment and excess capacity conditions in 1960 were derived and applied to the detailed occupational and industrial demands imposed by project construction. Through the application of these factors, the money costs of project construction were adjusted so as to more accurately reflect the foregone economic opportunities. The adjustment was made on both a national and regional basis.

The following are some of the more important results obtained from this analysis:

1) In the period from 1957–64, the opportunity costs imposed by public investments were significantly less than the amounts indicated by the money costs of such projects.

2) The pattern of responses by labor and capital markets to marginal demands in a period of less than full employment is a significant determinant of the extent of the cost adjustment required. This is shown by the different adjustments implied by the boundary and intermediate response functions in the national analysis.

3) The application of a uniform cost adjustment to all projects within a given program conceals significant difference among project types. As shown in Table 19, opportunity costs range from 69 to 95 per

cent of money costs depending on the specific project type under consideration and market response function used.

4) In much the same way, the geographic location of projects is an important variable. As Table 21 shows, the range of cost adjustment required as a single project type is assumed to be shifted among regions substantially exceeds the range of cost adjustment required when different project types are constructed in the same region.

5) Given the pattern of unemployed labor and capital resources in the 1957–64 period, cost estimates for project construction should have been reduced from 5 per cent to 30 per cent so as to reflect real costs. The appropriate reduction depends on the project type, the location of the construction site, and the market response functions.

UNEMPLOYMENT, EXCESS CAPACITY, AND BENEFIT-COST INVESTMENT CRITERIA $\boxed{V}$

THE PRIMARY PURPOSE of this study has been to examine the practical significance of the assumption of full employment which is implicit in nearly all benefit-cost analysis practiced until the present. To what extent is this assumption inimical to a correct evaluation of public investment projects in periods of less than full employment? As we have noted, all analysts agree in principle that adjustment of factor market prices is desirable in periods of depression with severe, widespread, and prolonged unemployment. To date, however, there has been no analysis of the extent of the adjustments required for such conditions. There are two additional forms of unemployment problems: (1) nonfrictional unemployment which persists nationally in spite of high and rising income and employment; and (2) high, geographically isolated, unemployment in a growing national economy. The conditions of the economy during the 1957–64 years illustrate the first of these two problems; Appalachia illustrates the second form.

Although this study was undertaken primarily to investigate the nature of cost adjustments for public investments during conditions of less than full employment, the process of examining the problem in detail uncovered a great deal about the anatomy of these investments. In fact, evidence on the composition of industrial, occupational, and regional impacts of these investments for some purposes may be as significant as the results related to its primary purpose.

Public investments in water resource development projects range from those in which there is no construction activity required, such as dredging, to those which involve the installation of huge capital facilities, such as large dams, reservoirs, and multiple-purpose appurtenances. There is substantial variation among these types of projects in the ratio of labor costs to total project costs, in the ratio of on-site labor cost to total labor cost, and in the distribution of the material, equipment, and supply demands imposed on the supporting industries. Heretofore, these differences have not been appreciated nor their relevance for policy perceived.

There are also significant differences in the pattern of occupational demands for water resource development projects and the occupational structure of the nation as a whole. For example, the total expenditure for labor compensation (direct and indirect) ranges from about 52 per cent of total costs for revetments to 72 per cent for large multiple-purpose projects. The proportion of labor compensation generated in producing a cross section of gross national product is 56 per cent, which falls near the lower extreme of this range. Accordingly, water resource development projects as a group represent a sector with a high employment ratio per dollar of expenditure.[1] At the same time, not all of the project types which have ratios of high labor cost to total cost have high ratios of *on-site labor* to total labor cost. The large multiple-purpose project, with labor accounting for 72 per cent of its total costs has a ratio of on-site labor cost to total labor cost of .58. Powerhouse construction, however, with 69 per cent of total costs accounted for by labor, has a ratio of on-site labor cost to total labor cost of only .25—about 75 per cent of labor costs appear as *off-site* payrolls in the industries on which powerhouse construction imposes material and equipment demands. Lock and concrete dam construction, with the third highest ratio of labor to total cost, shows over 60 per cent of total labor costs in off-site payrolls. Local flood protection works and dredging, on the other hand, with moderate to high ratios of labor to total cost, are respectively second and third in the ratio of on-site to total labor costs. These distinctions among project types are important for selecting investments which generate employment most appropriate for the two types of unemployment situations addressed in this study—that is, fairly uniform, geographically distributed, unemployment on the one hand, and geographically concentrated unemployment on the other.

The distribution of the industrial demands imposed by water resource development projects varies substantially among project types. While project construction imposes demands principally on the durable goods industries (for all project types except revetments),[2] the ratio of durable goods demand to gross material demands ranges from .2 to .65. Because of the cyclical sensitivity of durable goods output to changes in national income and output, the concentration of demands imposed by water resource development activities on this sector has substantial policy implications for conditions of less than full employment.

Similar inferences can be drawn from analysis of the occupational labor impact of water resource investment. During the period 1957–64,

---

[1] This is not to imply that water resource development projects are better in this respect than other public investments. In the public sector, there may be investments with higher ratios of labor compensation to total expenditure, or employment demands distributed more heavily toward the sensitive unemployment sectors. An analysis such as that undertaken in this study is required for all public investments in order to answer questions such as these.

[2] For revetments, the durable goods contribution (20 per cent of total industry output requirement) is equal to that for a cross section of gross national product. However, it is second to the mining sector (26 per cent), with quarrying operations the principal demand in this case.

the average unemployment rate weighted by project-generated labor costs was substantially higher than the national average unemployment rate. Hence, the probability that the labor used in these public invest-ments would be supplied from otherwise unemployed workers is higher than for a comparable expenditure for a cross section of gross national product. Given the conditions suggested by the unemployment history of the period 1957–64, investments in water resource facilities impose demands more selectively upon the heavily unemployed categories than an equal increase in general effective demand. Again, however, there should be no presumption that the water resource projects are peculiar in this regard within the public sector.

The labor demands imposed by water resource development activities are concentrated in three major occupational groups. The greatest de-mand is imposed on the category of craftsmen, foremen, and kindred workers. Typically, from one-third to two-fifths of total labor cost is represented by this category. While the entire category did not suffer unemployment rates higher than the national average during the 1957–64 period, the particular subclasses upon which water resource investment draws most heavily (such as construction craftsmen) ex-perienced an unemployment rate substantially above the national average. The second most significant occupational group is the opera-tives and kindred workers, which accounts for between 15 per cent and 30 per cent of total labor cost. This occupational category ex-perienced unemployment rates substantially higher than the national average during the 1957–64 period. The nonfarm unskilled laborers suffered the most acute unemployment conditions throughout the entire period 1957–64, with unemployment rates running as high as three to four times the national average. This occupational group accounts for about 10 per cent of total labor costs generated by the construction of water resource development projects.

Thus, the employment associated with water resource development tends to be drawn from the occupational categories with unemployment rates above the national average. And this type of labor demand is a confirmation that these construction activities are more effective em-ployment generators than, for example, an equivalent expenditure for a cross section of gross national product. On the other hand, the modest demands for unskilled workmen made by the construction of such projects is not promising from the point of view of chronically de-pressed areas which tend to be long on such manpower—even though unemployment rates in such areas are also high in the skilled trades and crafts required for project construction. Such questions, however, can be better dealt with by drawing on the regional model presented in Chapter III.

When a large multiple-purpose project is built in West Virginia (in Region VI, Lower Atlantic), the model predicts that some portion of the gross output demands are imposed on each of the ten regions of the nation. However, in spite of the regional preference functions built into the model, Region VI retains only 29 per cent of the gross output required by project construction. This compares with 44 per cent of retained gross demands in the case of a regional final demand of the composition of the gross national product.[3] At the same time, Regions II and III—Mid-Atlantic and East North Central—together account for about 43 per cent of the total because of the concentration of durable goods capacity and output in these regions. No other region contributes in excess of 6 per cent of the total. The local industries of Region VI which supply the bulk of the gross material, equipment, and supply requirements are in the trade and service sectors. Conversely, were the multiple-purpose project built in either Region II or Region III, 58 per cent and 70 per cent, respectively, of the gross output requirements would be retained in these regions. Construction of the multiple-purpose project in any of the other regions imposes almost a third of the gross output requirements on the region of project construction. Water resource investments for pile dikes, levees, and revetments impose a high proportion of the gross output requirements on the region of final demand (and, in this matter, correspond more to the GNP distribution).

The distribution of the off-site labor demands for water resource investments exhibits characteristics similar to the distribution of gross industry outputs. The off-site labor costs occasioned by the multiple-purpose project's gross output demands are somewhat greater than the labor costs associated with a gross output of the same size generated by a final demand of the composition of gross national product. In spite of this, the employment retained in the region of final demand is significantly greater in the case of the GNP vector than the retained employment associated with the water projects.

It should be noted that these statements refer only to the off-site employment; that is, the employment generated by expenditures for produced goods and services. The amount of wage and salary payments retained by each of the ten regions (when each is the site of construction) is 73 per cent or more of total labor costs *even among the regions which fail to retain a high proportion of the off-site labor compensation*, and rises to 90 per cent of the total in the East North Central Region. In part, the model attributes this large proportion of total labor cost to the region of project construction because of the assumption that all on-site labor is locally supplied—an assumption which may overstate the impact, particularly in the case of some highly skilled craftsmen.

---

[3] This, it should be noted, is production activity resulting from the first, second, and subsequent rounds of expenditures induced by the final expenditure.

In conclusion, it appears that water resource investments (and probably other public investments) generate more output and employment than an equivalent rise in effective demand of the composition of non-construction gross national product. Moreover, such public expenditures affect those sectors of the economy which are among the most sensitive to cyclical change.[4] Moreover, when the on-site labor impact is included, water resource investment in a depressed area distributes income and employment to the area in a significantly greater volume than would an increase of an equivalent amount in a final demand vector of the composition of the gross national product.

On the basis of this evidence, it is reasonable to expect that the social cost of public investment in water resource facilities is significantly overstated when market prices or contract costs are used to represent opportunity costs under conditions of less than full employment. In Chapter IV, we presented estimates of the extent to which nominal construction costs exceeded opportunity costs under conditions of national unemployment of about 5.5 per cent. It was argued there that, abstracting from regional impacts, substantial divergences between real and nominal costs arise when the conditions experienced during the 1957–64 period occur. Moreover, the variation in the divergence among project types is substantial. Thus, real labor costs for dredging or local flood protection projects are a significantly lower proportion of market labor costs (81 per cent and 85 per cent, respectively) than are the real labor costs of constructing a powerhouse or a large earth fill dam (91 per cent and 90 per cent, respectively). The divergence between the real and nominal costs of capital under similar circumstances appears to be only about half the variation found in connection with labor. Assuming our best-estimate response functions, real costs of capital range from 91 per cent for dredging and the construction of powerhouses to 96 per cent of contract costs for revetments.

Application of the response functions to the results obtained from the regional analysis demonstrates that variation among regions (with project type held constant) is greater than variation among project types (with regions held constant). Because of the inability to estimate excess industrial capacity by region, the analysis in this case was confined to differences caused only by variation in regional unemployment rates. Nevertheless, while the difference between real and nominal costs among project types ranged up to 11 percentage points, the variation by region ranged up to 25 percentage points. It should again be noted that the estimates presented in Chapter IV are based on the assumption that all on-site project labor is drawn from the region of project con-

---

[4] These statements apply to the construction phase only. Whether permanently increased employment will occur following construction is another question subject to analysis in its own right.

struction.[5] Despite the possibility of some resulting bias in the shadow factor estimates, however, the variation among regions is sufficiently great to warrant confidence that substantial differences in opportunity costs occur by reason of location and the unemployment rates relevant to specific areas (with project type held constant).

Given the estimated shadow costs, the question remains as to the extent to which the "nominal" benefit-cost ratios computed for projects constructed during the slack conditions between 1957–64, for example, or for chronically depressed areas, diverge from the more appropriate "opportunity cost" ratios.[6]

While nominal costs overstate opportunity costs by the magnitude suggested, the effect on the benefit-cost investment criterion will be dampened to the extent that costs in the benefit-cost formula represent operating, maintenance, and interim replacement costs as well as the capital (or construction) costs. It is convenient, although not essential, to assume that projects built under conditions of unemployment which exceed frictional levels are not necessarily destined to operate in a less than fully employed economy.[7] With this assumption, the component of annual project costs requiring adjustment will be only the capital charges—that is, the interest and amortization component of annual costs. The required adjustment in annual costs will be a function of the ratio of annual operating, maintenance, and interim replacement costs (which we designate as c) and the annual interest and amortization charges (designated as $a_{in}K$).

This is shown graphically in Figure 9. Here we show how the nominal benefit/cost ratio can diverge from the real B/C ratio for a range of capital intensities from $c/K = 0.01$ to $c/K = 0.10$ and $c/a_{in}K = 0.12$ to $c/a_{in}K = 2.5$ respectively.[8] Thus with a shadow factor of 1.0 (imply-

[5] It is recognized that insofar as the labor market area, particularly for the more highly skilled craftsmen and foremen, is likely to be larger than a single region, this assumption may to some extent bias the results in the direction implied by the ratio of the occupational unemployment rate in the project region to the corresponding rate outside of the region. This assumption also tends to overstate the extent to which project construction generates local employment.

[6] Our analysis has been directed to learning how much costs have been overstated when reliance is placed on factor market prices. The other relevant aspect for chronically depressed areas is: by how much have benefits been understated as a result of overlooking additional output by persons employed during the operations phase following construction who would have remained unemployed in the absence of the project? For a somewhat pessimistic view of this matter, see Roland McKean, *Efficiency in Government Through Systems Analysis* (New York: John Wiley and Sons, 1958), p. 161.

[7] If we wish to make the alternative assumption, the estimated future cost stream would have to be adjusted downward appropriately. For limitation on such adjustments, see Maynard M. Hufschmidt, John Krutilla, and Julius Margolis, Report of Panel of Consultants to the Bureau of the Budget, *Standards and Criteria for Formulating and Evaluating Federal Water Resources Development*, Washington, June 30, 1961, p. 32.

[8] Where $i = 3.25$ per cent and $n = 50$ years, and $i = 8$ per cent and $n = 50$ years,

FIGURE 9. RELATION OF ADJUSTED REAL TO NOMINAL BENEFIT/COST
RATIOS FOR DIFFERENT SHADOW FACTORS AND CAPITAL INTENSITIES

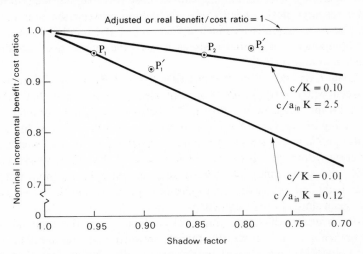

ing full employment), the nominal B/C ratio[9] will be identical to the
real B/C ratio irrespective of differences in capital intensities among
projects. With shadow factors of less than 1.0 (implying less than full
employment), the nominal B/C ratio associated with any given ratio
of operating, maintenance, and replacement costs to annual capital
charges diverges from the real B/C ratio in proportion to the decline
in shadow factor (increase in the unemployment rate). For projects
with annual operating, maintenance, and replacement costs (c) equal
to about 12 per cent of the annual capital charges ($a_{in}K$), the nominal
B/C ratio could get as low as 0.70:1 and yet represent a real B/C ratio
of unity with the shadow factor within the approximate range estimated
in this study. For any given ratio of annual operating cost to annual
capital charge ($c/a_{in}K = 2.5$), the locus of points given by varying the
shadow factors trace the lower bound of the nominal B/C ratio that is
still consistent with a real B/C ratio of unity. Thus points P_1 and P_2 on
the two lines (nominal B/C ratio of 0.95:1) correspond to the minimum
nominal B/C ratios for two combinations of capital intensities and unemployment conditions that are still economically acceptable. Any points
such as P_1' and P_2' in the wedge between the nominal B/C boundary lines
and the horizontal line (where the adjusted or real B/C ratio equals
one) represents a real B/C ratio exceeding unity despite its fractional

---

respectively. The low interest rate is associated with a high c/K ($= 0.10$) and the
high rate with the low c/K ($= 0.01$) to bracket the relevant range for $c/a_{in}K$
in Figure 9.
[9] It should be understood that we are talking in the present context of *marginal* or
incremental benefit/cost ratios, and thus the average benefit/cost ratios would
exceed unity in the relevant range.

nominal B/C ratio. Given the potential differences in the ratio of annual operating cost to annual capital cost possible between different water resource developments, the divergence between the nominal and the real B/C ratios is as much a function of the relation between the two components of annual costs as it is of the employment conditions considered in this study.[10]

What, then, does this computation tell us? First, by differentiating between water resource development types, we discover that there is a significant range in the divergence between real and nominal costs, depending on the type of project. If there is such variation within a particular public works subset, it is highly probable that there is even greater variation within, and between, other subsets of the public works sector. While the significance of these results is self-evident, their practical value is limited until additional types of expenditures in the public sector have been similarly investigated.

Moreover, by disaggregating project demands to the regional level, a significant range in the divergence between real and nominal costs was noted. This was caused by the uneven distribution of resource demands and patterns of unemployment regionally. Investigating subnational aggregates to the extent that depressed areas can be isolated for more discriminating treatment will yield still more precise information on the extent of, and particular reasons for, the overstatement of costs relative to true opportunity costs. Regional specificity, just as distinguishing among project types, adds a dimension to our understanding of the nature of the problem.

Finally, the capital intensity of the expenditures under consideration has significance of its own for changing the ranking of alternatives under conditions of less than full employment. Assume, on the one hand, that we are considering unemployment of a short-run nature which may extend over the construction period (months) but not persist into the operating phase of the project. In this case, the higher the ratio of annual capital charges to annual operating costs, the greater the significance of the cost adjustment by reason of the existence of otherwise idle resources during the construction period. If, on the other hand, we are talking about a chronically depressed area from which operating personnel as well as construction workers are drawn, the relative capital intensity of projects will have less significance for changing project rankings as a result of taking unemployed resources explicitly into our calculations.

In conclusion, we should emphasize that such cost adjustments as

---

[10] It should be recalled that the range in the relation between annual operating and annual capital costs was obtained not only by the differences in c/K, but also by associating the lower interest charge (3.25 per cent) with the highest operating cost to capital ratio ($c/K = 0.10$) and the highest interest charge (8 per cent) with the lowest operating cost to capital ratio ($c/K = 0.01$).

have been described are essential for a more discriminating choice among all alternatives available in the public sector. We hope that the results of this study will prompt similar analyses for all of the types of public expenditures. This is essential if information of comparable nature is to be developed for the entire public sector. In the absence of such an undertaking, our study might appear to be a brief for a particular kind of public works program. That is not the intention. Indeed, this analysis has been prepared specifically to present the conceptual model, computer programs, and computational methods which can facilitate carrying out such studies over the entire range of public expenditure.

MATHEMATICAL FORMULATION OF NATIONAL SECTORAL DEMAND MODEL

THE NATIONAL MODEL of sectoral demand described below contains Z occupational categories and N industries. Each industry produces a homogeneous output by combining factor inputs with purchased inputs from other industries. In the model, all exchanged commodities and services are measured in physical units and evaluated at base-year prices. In the notational glossary, capital letters represent matrices and lower case letters represent vectors. Matrix and vector dimensions are stated in parentheses.

NOTATIONAL GLOSSARY

f—total cost for project construction.

u—row vector consisting of all ones, of appropriate dimensionality.

y—column vector $(N \times 1)$ of final demand for materials, equipment, and supplies required from each industry as inputs into project construction.

t_2—column vector $(Z \times 1)$ of total on-site labor cost for project construction, by occupational category.

g—contractor's profit and overhead and other project costs not included in either on-site labor cost or expenditures for materials, equipment, and supplies.

x—column vector $(N \times 1)$ of the gross output level of each industry required by the final demand.

A—square matrix $(N \times N)$ of input-output coefficients which define the source and quantity of inputs to each industry per dollar's worth of output from that industry.

E—diagonal matrix $(N \times N)$ of the total man-year labor requirements per dollar's worth of gross output in each industry.

j—column vector $(N \times 1)$ of total man-year labor requirements for each industry required by the final demand.

B—rectangular matrix $(Z \times N)$ containing labor coefficients which define the volume of man-year occupational requirements in each industry per unit of man-year labor requirements in that industry.

97

m—column vector $(Z \times 1)$ of total man-year labor requirements for each occupational category required by the final demand.

W—diagonal matrix $(Z \times Z)$ of average annual wage and salary income, by occupational category.

t_1'—column vector $(Z \times 1)$ of total off-site labor cost generated by the final demand, by occupational category.

X—diagonal matrix $(N \times N)$ of the gross output level of each industry required by the final demand; vector x transformed into a diagonal matrix.

$e, r, c,$ i, p, q—six column vectors $(N \times 1)$ of ratios of value-added components (respectively, employee compensation, net interest, capital consumption allowances, indirect business taxes, corporate profits, and proprietor and rental income) to gross output by industry.

$e_1, r_1, c_1,$ i_1, p_1, q_1—six column vectors $(N \times 1)$ of value-added components (respectively, employee compensation, net interest, capital consumption allowances, indirect business taxes, corporate profits, and proprietor and rental income) generated by the final demand by industry.

C—rectangular matrix $(N \times 6)$ defined by $[e, r, c, i, p, q]$.

D—rectangular matrix $(N \times 6)$ defined by $[e_1, r_1, c_1, i_1, p_1, q_1]$.

t_1—column vector $(Z \times 1)$ of total off-site employee compensation (adjusted) generated by the final demand, by occupational category.

t_*—column vector $(Z \times 1)$ of total labor income generated in each occupational category, by project construction.

THE NATIONAL SECTORAL DEMAND MODEL

The total expenditure for project construction is divided into (a) on-site employee compensation, (b) final expenditures for material, equipment, and supplies, and (c) contractor's profit, overhead, and other project costs not included in (a) and (b).

$$f = ut_2 + uy + g. \tag{1}$$

The gross output of each industry generated by the final demand is equal to the product of the final demand for materials, equipment, and supplies by industry and the inverse of the interindustry technical coefficient matrix.

$$x = (I - A)^{-1} \cdot y. \tag{2}$$

Total man-year labor requirements by industry (j) are derived by applying the appropriate labor coefficients (E) to the gross output levels (x) derived above, i.e.,

$$j = E \cdot x. \tag{3}$$

These man-year labor requirements are disaggregated into detailed occupational categories by applying the appropriate occupational coefficients to the total industry labor demands.

$$m = B \cdot j. \tag{4}$$

The occupational breakdown of generated labor income is obtained by applying average annual occupational wage and salary income estimates to the occupational man-year labor requirements.

$$t_1' = W \cdot m. \tag{5}$$

The value of the value-added components generated by the final demand for materials, equipment, and supplies, by industry, is the product of the gross industrial outputs and the appropriate ratios of value-added components to gross output.

$$D = X \cdot C. \tag{6}$$

To equate the estimates of total labor income obtained through the occupational man-year procedure (equation 5) with the estimates of labor income obtained through the value-added component procedure (equation 6), the occupational breakdown obtained in equation 5 is adjusted by the ratio of the total employee compensation figure secured in equation 6 to the total wage and salary income figure generated through equation 5.

$$t_1 = (u \cdot e_1 / u \cdot t_1') \cdot t_1'. \tag{7}$$

The total employee compensation generated by the expenditure for project construction, by occupational category, is the sum of the occupational distribution of off-site and on-site employee compensation.

$$t_* = t_1 + t_2. \tag{8}$$

By definitional accounting identities, the value of a final expenditure is equal to the sum of the value-added components which enter its production.

$$uy = ue_1 + ur_1 + uc_1 + ui_1 + up_1 + uq_1. \tag{9}$$

$$uy = ut_1 + ur_1 + uc_1 + ui_1 + up_1 + uq_1. \tag{10}$$

WATER RESOURCE PROJECTS GENERATING BASIC COST DATA

THE DATA analyzed in this study refer to the following twelve types of public water development projects, for which the names and locations of individual projects are listed.

Large Earth Fill Dams

Painted Rock Dam	Arizona

Small Earth Fill Dams

Buckhorn Reservoir	Kentucky
Dillon Reservoir (clearing)	Ohio
Mansfield Reservoir	Indiana

Local Flood Protection

Big Dalton Wash Channel	California
Cape Girardeau	Missouri
Woonsocket, Blackstone River	Rhode Island

Pile Dikes

Ackley Bend to Leavenworth Reach, Missouri River	Kansas
Ashport-Goldust, Mississippi River	Arkansas
Miami to Glasgow Bend, Missouri River	Missouri
Near Bigelow, Arkansas River	Arkansas
New Haven Reach to Weldon Spring Bend, Missouri River	Missouri

Levees

Elk Chute Drainage District	Missouri
Lake Ponchartrain	Louisiana
Near Muscatine, Mississippi River	Iowa
Old Lake	Louisiana
Ripley, Mississippi River	Tennessee
Santa Maria Valley and Bradford Canyon	California
Yazoo River	Mississippi

Revetments
   Arkansas River Revetment   Arkansas
   Bank Paving, Mississippi River   Missouri, Tennessee,
                                        Arkansas, Mississippi

   Board Revetment, Red River   Louisiana
   Cessions to Kempe Bend,   Mississippi, Arkansas,
      Mississippi River   Louisiana
   Sacramento River Bank Protection California

Powerhouse Construction
   Beaver Dam Powerhouse   Arkansas

Medium Concrete Dams
   Beaver Dam and Reservoir   Arkansas

Lock and Concrete Dams
   Columbia Lock and Dam   Alabama

Large Multiple-Purpose Projects
   Glen Canyon Dam and Powerhouse   Arizona

Dredging
   Anacostia River   District of Columbia
   Atlantic Intra-Coastal Waterway, South Carolina
      Port Royal Sound
   Bronx River   New York
   Brunswick Harbor   Georgia
   Calumet-Sag Channel   Illinois
   Columbia River between Bonneville Washington, Oregon
      and Vancouver
   Duxburg Harbor   Massachusetts
   Galveston Harbor   Texas
   Gulf Intra-Coastal Waterway,   Texas
      Freeport
   Intra-Coastal Waterway,   Florida
      Caloosahatchie River to
      Anclote River
   Manteo to Oregon Inlet   North Carolina
   Matagorda Channel, Point Lavaca   Texas
   New York Harbor   New York
   Philadelphia, Delaware River   Pennsylvania
   Sabine-Neches Waterway   Texas

Miscellaneous
   Bayou Macon Channel Improvement   Louisiana
   Jetties, Gold Beach   Oregon
   Outlet Channel, Sardis Dam   Mississippi
   Sea Wall Extension, Galveston   Texas

DETAILED OCCUPATIONAL CATEGORIES

THE OCCUPATIONAL CATEGORIES with which this analysis has been concerned are aggregates of the following detailed categories used in the industry-occupational matrix of the Bureau of Labor Statistics of the U.S. Department of Labor.

PROFESSIONAL, TECHNICAL, AND KINDRED WORKERS

Engineers, Technical
1. Engineers, aeronautical
2. Engineers, chemical
3. Engineers, civil
4. Engineers, electrical
5. Engineers, industrial
6. Engineers, mechanical
7. Engineers, metallurgical, etc.
8. Engineers, mining
9. Engineers, sales
10. Other engineers, technical

Medical and Other Health Workers
11. Dentists
12. Dietitians and nutritionists
13. Nurses, professional
14. Nurses, student
15. Optometrists
16. Osteopaths
17. Pharmacists
18. Physicians and surgeons
19. Psychologists
20. Technicians, medical and dental
21. Chiropractors and therapists
22. Veterinarians

Teachers
23. Teachers, elementary
24. Teachers, secondary
25. Teachers, other except college
26. Teachers, college

Natural Scientists
27. Chemists
28. Agricultural scientists
29. Biological scientists
30. Geologists and geophysicists
31. Mathematicians
32. Physicists
33. Other natural scientists

Social scientists
34. Economists
35. Statisticians and actuaries
36. Other social scientists

Technicians, except medical and dental
37. Draftsmen
38. Air traffic controllers
39. Radio operators
40. Surveyors

41. Technicians, electrical and electronic
42. Technicians, other engineering and physical scientists
43. Technicians, other

Other Professional, Technical, and Kindred
44. Accountants and auditors
45. Airplane pilots and navigators
46. Architects

47. Designers, except design draftsmen
48. Foresters and conservationists
49. Lawyers and judges
50. Librarians
51. Artists, athletes, entertainers
52. Personnel and labor relations workers
53. Social and welfare workers
54. Professional, technical, and kindred workers, NEC

MANAGERS, OFFICIALS, AND PROPRIETORS

55. Managers, officials, and proprietors, NEC
56. Conductors, railroad

57. Officers, pilots, ship engineers

CLERICAL AND KINDRED WORKERS

Stenographers, Typists, and Secretaries
58. Stenographers
59. Typists
60. Secretaries

Office Machine Operators
61. Billing and bookkeeping machine operators
62. Key punch operators
63. Tabulating machine operators

64. Other office machine operators

Other Clerical and Kindred Workers
65. Bank tellers
66. Accounting clerks
67. Payroll and time keeping clerks
68. Telephone operators
69. Clerical and kindred workers, NEC

SALES WORKERS

70. Sales workers

CRAFTSMEN, FOREMEN, AND KINDRED WORKERS

Construction Craftsmen
71. Carpenters
72. Brickmason, stone, tile setters
73. Cement and concrete finishers

74. Electricians
75. Excavating, grading, machine operators
76. Painters and paperhangers
77. Plasterers
78. Plumbers and pipefitters

79. Roofers and slaters
80. Structural metal workers
81. Foremen, NEC

Metalworking Craftsmen
82. Machinists, production and toolroom
83. Machinists, maintenance
84. Boilermakers
85. Blacksmiths, forge, hammermen
86. Heat treaters, annealers, etc.
87. Millwrights
88. Molders, metal (except covermakers)
89. Patternmakers, metal and wood
90. Rollers and roll hands
91. Tinsmiths
92. Toolmakers and diemakers
93. Assemblers, metalworking, Class A
94. Inspectors, metalworking, Class A
95. Electroplaters
96. Machine tool operators, Class A

Mechanics and Repairmen
97. Motor vehicle mechanics
98. Air conditioning, heating, refrigeration mechanics
99. Airplane mechanics and repairmen
100. Office machine mechanics
101. Radio and television mechanics
102. Railroad and car shop mechanics

103. Other mechanics and repairmen

Selected Printing Trades Craftsmen
104. Compositors and typesetters
105. Electrotypers and stereotypers
106. Engravers, except photoengravers
107. Photoengravers, lithographers
108. Pressmen and plate printers

Selected Skilled Occupations—
Transportation, Public Utilities
109. Line and servicemen, telephone and power
110. Locomotive engineers
111. Locomotive firemen

Other Craftsmen and Kindred Workers
112. Bakers
113. Cabinetmakers
114. Cranemen, derrickmen, hoistmen
115. Glaziers
116. Inspectors, log and lumber
117. Inspectors, other
118. Jewelers and watchmakers
119. Loom fixers
120. Millers
121. Opticians, lens grinders, etc.
122. Stationary engineers
123. Turbine operators, light, etc.
124. Craftsmen and kindred workers, NEC

OPERATIVES AND KINDRED WORKERS

125. Asbestos–insulation workers
126. Apprentices

127. Assemblers, metalworking, Class B

128. Inspectors, metalworking, Class B
129. Furnacemen, smelters, pourers
130. Heaters, metal
131. Welders and flame cutters
132. Machine tool operators, metalworking, Class B
133. Electroplater helpers
134. Drivers, bus, truck, tractor
135. Delivery, routemen, cab drivers
136. Brakemen and switchmen, railroad
137. Power station operators
138. Sailors and deck hands
139. Knitters, loopers, and toppers
140. Sewers and stitchers
141. Spinners, textile
142. Weavers, textile
143. Mine operatives, laborers, NEC
144. Blasters and powdermen
145. Meatcutters, except meat packing
146. Operatives and kindred workers, NEC

SERVICE WORKERS

147. Private household workers

Protective Service Workers
148. Firemen
149. Guards, watchmen, doorkeepers
150. Policemen, detectives, etc.

151. Cooks, except private household
152. Bartenders, counter and fountain workers
153. Waiters and waitresses
154. Other service workers

LABORERS

155. Laborers, except farm

FARMERS

156. Farmers and farm workers

NEC means not elsewhere classified.

MATHEMATICAL FORMULATION OF THE REGIONAL SECTORAL DEMAND MODEL

THE MULTIREGIONAL MODEL described below, like the national model described in Appendix 1, contains Z occupational categories and N industries. Each industry produces a homogeneous output by combining factor inputs with purchased inputs from other industries. The industries are divided into Type A of which there are a, Type B of which there are b, Type C of which there are c, and Local of which there are d. ($a + b + c = q$.) Each of these industries and occupations is present in each of S regions of the country. In the notational glossary, capital letters (other than Z, S, and N) represent matrices and lower case letters (other than a, b, c, and d) represent vectors or scalars. In the interest of reduced notation, column vectors which are placed in diagonal matrix form for computational purposes are denoted by this hat symbol: $\hat{\ }$. For example,

$$a = \begin{bmatrix} a_1 \\ a_2 \\ a_3 \end{bmatrix}, \quad \hat{a} = \begin{bmatrix} a_1 & 0 & 0 \\ 0 & a_2 & 0 \\ 0 & 0 & a_3 \end{bmatrix}.$$

Matrix and vector dimensions are stated in parentheses.

NOTATIONAL GLOSSARY

s^*—the region in which the final demand is assumed to be imposed.

s—designation of any one of the S individual regions.

$$x = \begin{bmatrix} x_\alpha \\ \hline x_\beta \\ \hline x_\gamma \\ \hline x_\delta \end{bmatrix}$$ —column vector ($N \times 1$) of the gross output level of each industry required by the final demand, partitioned into:

x_α—column vector ($a \times 1$) of the gross output level of the Type A industries,

x_β—column vector ($b \times 1$) of the gross output level of the Type B industries,

x_γ—column vector $(c \times 1)$ of the gross output level of the Type C industries, and

x_δ—column vector $(d \times 1)$ of the gross output level of the Local industries.

$$y = \begin{bmatrix} y_a \\ \hline y_\beta \\ \hline y_\gamma \\ \hline y_\delta \end{bmatrix}$$—column vector $(N \times 1)$ of the final demand for materials, equipment, and supplies, by industry, partitioned into:

y_a—column vector $(a \times 1)$ of the final demand for materials, equipment, and supplies for Type A industries,

y_β—column vector $(b \times 1)$ of the final demand for materials, equipment, and supplies for Type B industries,

y_γ—column vector $(c \times 1)$ of the final demand for materials, equipment, and supplies for Type C industries, and

y_δ—column vector $(d \times 1)$ of the final demand for materials, equipment, and supplies for Local industries.

$$X_*^S = \begin{bmatrix} X_a^S \\ \hline X_\beta^S \\ \hline X_\gamma^S \\ \hline X_\delta^S \end{bmatrix}$$—rectangular matrix $(N \times S)$ each column of which shows the gross output required of each industry in one particular region, partitioned into:

X_a^S—rectangular matrix $(a \times S)$ each column of which shows the gross output levels of all Type A industries in one particular region,

X_β^S—rectangular matrix $(b \times S)$ each column of which shows the gross output levels of all Type B industries in one particular region,

X_γ^S—rectangular matrix $(c \times S)$ each column of which shows the gross output levels of all Type C industries in one particular region, and

X_δ^S—rectangular matrix $(d \times S)$ each column of which shows the gross output level of all Local industries in one particular region.

$$H^S = \begin{bmatrix} H_a^S \\ \hline H_\beta^S \\ \hline H_\gamma^S \end{bmatrix}$$—rectangular matrix $[(a + b + c) \times S]$ of regional distribution coefficients each column of which describes the fraction of the total output of each of the national industries produced in one of the S regions, partitioned into:

H_a^S—rectangular matrix $(a \times S)$ of coefficients each column of which (H_a^s) describes the fraction of the total national output of each of the Type A industries produced in one of the S regions,

H_β^s—rectangular matrix ($b \times S$) of coefficients each column of which (H_β^s) describes the fraction of the total national output of each of the Type B industries produced in one of the S regions, and

H_γ^s—rectangular matrix ($c \times S$) of coefficients each column of which (H_γ^s) describes the fraction of the total national output of each of the Type C industries produced in one of the S regions.

θ—a scalar representing the regional preference function for Type B industries.

λ—a scalar representing the regional preference function for Type C industries.

k_β^s—column vector ($b \times 1$) of the final demand of Type B industries allocated to the region wherein the project is constructed, because of regional preference.

k_γ^s—column vector ($c \times 1$) of the final demand of Type C industries allocated to the region wherein the project is constructed, because of regional preference.

R_β^S—rectangular matrix ($b \times S$) each column of which shows the portion of gross output of Type B industries allocated to a particular region by the regional distribution coefficients.

R_γ^S—rectangular matrix ($c \times S$) each column of which shows the portion of gross output of Type C industries allocated to a particular region by the regional distribution coefficients.

K_β^S—rectangular matrix ($b \times S$) with the sth column $= k_\beta^s$ and the remaining columns null vectors.

K_γ^S—rectangular matrix ($c \times S$) with the sth column $= k_\gamma^s$ and the remaining columns null vectors.

A_{dq}—rectangular matrix $[d \times (a + b + c)]$ of input-output coefficients describing flows from Local industries to national industries.

A_{dd}—square matrix ($d \times d$) of input-output coefficients describing flows from Local industries to Local industries.

L^S—rectangular matrix ($d \times S$) each column of which shows the final demands imposed on the Local industries of a particular region by the national industries in that region.

Y_δ^S—rectangular matrix $(d \times S)$ with the sth column containing y_δ, the final demands imposed by the project on the Local industries wherein the project is located, and the remaining columns null vectors.

L_*^S—rectangular matrix $(d \times S)$ each column of which shows the total "final" output requirement on the Local industries of a particular region due to project construction.

J^S—rectangular matrix $(N \times S)$ each column of which shows the total man-year labor requirements for a particular region, by industry.

E—diagonal matrix $(N \times N)$ of the total man-year labor requirements per dollar's worth of gross output in each industry.

M^S—rectangular matrix $(Z \times S)$ each column of which shows the total man-year labor requirements for a particular region, by occupation.

B—rectangular matrix $(Z \times N)$ containing labor coefficients which define the volume of man-year occupational requirements in each industry per unit of man-year labor requirements in that industry.

T_1^S—rectangular matrix $(Z \times S)$ each column of which shows the off-site employee compensation generated in each occupational category by the final demand for a particular region.

A—square matrix $(N \times N)$ of input-output coefficients of all national and Local industries.

W—diagonal matrix $(Z \times Z)$ of adjusted average annual wage and salary income by occupational category.

T_2^S—rectangular matrix $(Z \times S)$ with the sth column containing the occupational on-site labor cost which is assigned to the region wherein the project is constructed and the remaining columns null vectors.

T_*^S—rectangular matrix $(Z \times S)$ each column of which shows the total employee compensation generated in each occupational category for a particular region.

REGIONAL SECTORAL DEMAND MODEL

The function of this regional allocation model is the distribution of the gross industrial and occupational demands generated by project construction among the regions of the country according to the regional preference properties already noted. It will be recalled that gross output by industry sector equals the product of the final demand for materials, equipment, and supplies by industry and the inverse of the input-output technical coefficient matrix.

$$x = (I - A)^{-1} \cdot y \qquad (1)$$

These gross outputs, by industry, are allocated among regions as follows:

Type A outputs: The gross output of the truly national, or Type A, industries is distributed among the S regions according to the proportion of the industry's national output which is supplied by the region.

$$X_a^S = \hat{x}_a \cdot H_a^S \qquad (2)$$

Type B outputs: A portion of the final demand of the Type B industries is allocated to the region wherein the project is constructed on the basis of the appropriate regional preference function.

$$\hat{y}_\beta \cdot (H_\beta^s \cdot \theta) = k_\beta^s \text{ for } s = s^* \qquad (3)$$

The nonallocated portion of the gross outputs of Type B industries is distributed among the S regions on the basis of Type A regional distribution coefficients.

$$(\hat{x}_\beta - \hat{k}_\beta^s) \cdot H_\beta^S = R_\beta^S \qquad (4)$$

The regional preference shown to the region wherein the project is constructed (augmented by $S - 1$ null vectors) is then added to the appropriate regional output vectors obtained in equation 4 to yield the entire regional distribution of Type B gross outputs.

$$R_\beta^S + K_\beta^S = X_\beta^S \qquad (5)$$

Type C outputs: The gross outputs of Type C industries are allocated among the S regions through the same allocation procedure shown in equations 3, 4, and 5. The Type C industry preference function (λ) is substituted for (θ).

$$\hat{y}_\gamma \cdot (H_\gamma^s \cdot \lambda) = k_\gamma^s \qquad (6)$$

$$(\hat{x}_\gamma - \hat{k}_\gamma^s) \cdot H_\gamma^S = R_\gamma^S \qquad (7)$$

$$R_\gamma^S + K_\gamma^S = X_\gamma^S \qquad (8)$$

Local outputs: The Local industry outputs required in each of the S regions to satisfy the production requirements of the national industry outputs in each region are defined by the product of the national industry gross outputs in each region and the technical coefficients describing flows from Local industries to national industries.

$$A_{dq} \cdot \begin{bmatrix} X_a^S \\ \hline X_\beta^S \\ \hline X_\gamma^S \end{bmatrix} = L^S \qquad (9)$$

The final demand levied by the project on Local industries in the project region is added to the output demands on these Local industries by the interindustry requirements of Type A, Type B, and Type C industries in the region (L^S) to give the total "final" output requirements for the Local industries in the region.

$$L^S + Y^S_\delta = L^S_*$$ (10)

The gross output of the Local industries in each region equals the product of the Local industry "final" output requirements and the inverse of the Local-to-Local technical coefficient matrix.

$$(I - A_{dd})^{-1} \cdot L^S_* = X^S_\delta$$ (11)

Now the amount of each good produced in each region has been estimated. The remainder of the model is concerned with the calculation of the labor and other value-added components, as in Appendix 1, equations 3 through 8.

The total man-year labor requirements for any region required by the final demand for materials, equipment, and supplies, by industry, is obtained by multiplying the regionally distributed gross outputs of each industry by the ratios of man-year to output for each industry.

$$J^S = E \cdot X^S_*$$ (12)

The occupational breakdown of these labor requirements, by region, is defined by the product of the industry breakdown obtained in equation 12 and the occupation-by-industry matrix.

$$M^S = B \cdot J^S$$ (13)

The adjusted occupational employee compensation generated by the final demand for materials, equipment, and supplies, by region, is the product of the adjusted average annual occupational wage and salary income estimates and the regional man-year labor requirements, by occupation, derived in equation 13.

$$T^S_1 = W \cdot M^S$$ (14)

The total occupational labor income generated by the project, both on-site and off-site, by region, is obtained by adding the on-site occupational labor income assigned to the region wherein the project is constructed to the regional distribution of off-site occupational income generated by the final demand for materials, equipment, and supplies.

$$T^S_* = T^S_1 + T^S_2$$ (15)

Represented in X^S_* and T^S_*, then, is the regional breakdown of both the gross outputs by industry and the total labor costs by occupation.

PROOF OF MATHEMATICAL CONSISTENCY OF NATIONAL AND REGIONAL SECTORAL DEMAND MODELS

A REGIONAL INPUT-OUTPUT MODEL describes the allocation of gross output to ten regions. The calculation requires a separate treatment for national industries and Local industries. It is proved below that the U.S. totals of gross output by industry are consistent with the sums of the ten regions.

$A = [a_{ij}]$ matrix (82×82) of input-output coefficients.

Partition into $q = a + b + c$ national industries and d Local industries

$$\begin{bmatrix} A_{11} & A_{12} \\ A_{21} & A_{22} \end{bmatrix}$$

where A_{21} is $d \times q$ Local-to-national industry set of coefficients and A_{22} is $d \times d$ Local-to-Local industry set of coefficients, etc., $y =$ vector of final demands (82×1), $y_1 =$ national industry final demands ($q \times 1$), $y_2 =$ Local industry final demands ($d \times 1$).

To calculate x vector of gross industry outputs (82×1) including $x_1(q \times 1)$, national industry gross outputs, and $x_2(d \times 1)$, Local industry gross outputs, the standard 82-sector input-output calculation is

$$x = [I - A]^{-1} \cdot y.$$

Partitioning into national and Local industries

$$\begin{bmatrix} x_1 \\ x_2 \end{bmatrix} = \begin{bmatrix} I_q - A_{11} & -A_{12} \\ -A_{21} & I_d - A_{22} \end{bmatrix}^{-1} \cdot \begin{bmatrix} y_1 \\ y_2 \end{bmatrix}.$$

For notational simplicity let

$$G_{11} = I_q - A_{11}$$
$$G_{12} = -A_{12}$$
$$G_{21} = -A_{21} \qquad (1)$$
$$G_{22} = I_d - A_{22} \qquad (2)$$

$$\begin{bmatrix} x_1 \\ x_2 \end{bmatrix} = \begin{bmatrix} G_{11} & G_{12} \\ G_{21} & G_{22} \end{bmatrix}^{-1} \cdot \begin{bmatrix} y_1 \\ y_2 \end{bmatrix}.$$

After the 82×82 matrix inversion, the inverse matrix may be partitioned as before between national and Local industries

$$\begin{bmatrix} x_1 \\ x_2 \end{bmatrix} = \begin{bmatrix} F_{11} & F_{12} \\ F_{21} & F_{22} \end{bmatrix} \cdot \begin{bmatrix} y_1 \\ y_2 \end{bmatrix}.$$

By definition: $G \cdot F = I$, where G is the partitioned matrix of $I - A$ and F is the partitioned matrix of the inverse of G

$$\begin{bmatrix} G_{11} & G_{12} \\ G_{21} & G_{22} \end{bmatrix} \cdot \begin{bmatrix} F_{11} & F_{12} \\ F_{21} & F_{22} \end{bmatrix} = \begin{bmatrix} I_q & 0 \\ 0 & I_d \end{bmatrix}.$$

By multiplying the second row in the G matrix times the first and second columns in the F matrix, we develop two matrix equations below which will be useful later in the analysis:

$$G_{21}\ F_{11} + G_{22}\ F_{21} = 0 \tag{3}$$

$$G_{21}\ F_{12} + G_{22}\ F_{22} = I_d. \tag{4}$$

Also note the matrix expressions for gross output by national industry and gross output by Local industry

$$x_1 = F_{11}\ y_1 + F_{12}\ y_2 \tag{5}$$

$$x_2 = F_{21}\ y_1 + F_{22}\ y_2. \tag{6}$$

Equations 1 through 6 summarize the results of the national input-output calculations which will be useful in understanding the regional analysis.

The computer methodology for regional analysis operates differently. For the national industries, x_1 is given as the national input-output calculation described in equation 5 above; and then is distributed regionally according to the region in which the final demand is assumed to be imposed, the particular regional preference function, and the regional distribution coefficients.[1] Having derived gross output for the national industries of a region, x_1^s, this is multiplied by the matrix of Local-to-national industry input-output coefficients to estimate the production requirements imposed upon Local industries by the gross output of national industries.

$$L^s = A_{21}\ x_1^s. \tag{7}$$

The total "final" output requirement for Local industry is the above vector plus the final demand for Local industry output levied directly by the project. The latter is presumed to be zero for all regions other than the region in which the project is assumed to be located.

$$y_2^s = y_2 \text{ for } s = s^* \text{ (home region)}$$

$$y_2^s = 0 \text{ for } s \neq s^*.$$

The final computational step is to multiply total "final" output requirements for Local industries by the inverse Local-to-Local industry input-

[1] Further explained in footnote 7, Appendix 6.

output matrix to derive gross Local industry output by region, L_*^s. This is expressed below as a computation for each region.

$$L_*^s = (I_d - A_{22})^{-1} (L^s + y_2^s) \qquad s = 1, 2 \dots S. \tag{8}$$

Substituting equation 7 into equation 8, we derive:

$$L_*^s = (I_d - A_{22})^{-1} (A_{21} x_1^s + y_2^s) \quad s = 1, 2 \dots S. \tag{9}$$

We must now prove that the sum of regional gross outputs calculated above,

$$\sum_{s=1}^{S} L_*^s,$$

will equal x_2 calculated in the national (82×82) matrix calculation (equation 6).

Summing vertically the S equations of equation 9, we derive

$$\sum L_*^s = (I_d - A_{22})^{-1} (A_{21} x_1 + y_2). \tag{10}$$

This is easily seen since

$$x_1 = \sum x_1^s \text{ and } y_2 = \sum y_2^s.$$

Substitute equations 1 and 2 into equation 10:

$$\sum L_*^s = G_{22}^{-1}(-G_{21} x_1 + y_2). \tag{11}$$

Substituting for x_1 in equation 11 from equation 5,

$$\sum L_*^s = G_{22}^{-1}[-G_{21}(F_{11} y_1 + F_{12} y_2) + y_2]. \tag{12}$$

Collecting terms on y_1 and y_2

$$\sum L_*^s = [G_{22}^{-1}(-G_{21})F_{11}] y_1 + [G_{22}^{-1}\{(-G_{21})F_{12} + I\}]y_2. \tag{13}$$

Solve equation 3 for F_{21}:

$$F_{21} = G_{22}^{-1}(-G_{21})F_{11} = \text{coefficient of } y_1 \text{ in equation 13.} \tag{14}$$

Solve equation 4 for F_{22}:

$$F_{22} = G_{22}^{-1}(I_d - G_{21} F_{12}) = G_{22}^{-1}(-G_{21} F_{12} + I) = \tag{15}$$
$$\text{coefficient of } y_2 \text{ in equation 13.}$$

Therefore, substituting equations 14 and 15 into equation 13,

$$\sum L_*^s = F_{21} y_1 + F_{22} y_2. \tag{16}$$

Thus, the sum across regions of gross output for Local industries may be expressed as in equation 16. As may be seen from equation 6, this is the matrix multiplication of the appropriate partitioned elements of the inverse 82×82 input-output matrix to calculate x_2. Therefore $\sum L_*^s = x_2$, and the regional calculation is consistent with the national totals.

COMPUTER PROCESS FOR SECTORAL
DEMAND AND SHADOW COST MODELS

UNDERSTANDING OF THE METHODOLOGY described in the models of Chapters II, III and IV and expressed as a series of matrix operations in Appendices 1, 4 and 9, can be increased by a description of the computer process by which the bill of final demands imposed by an expenditure is transformed into the analytical tables appearing throughout the text. In the description of the computer process, the possibility of further applications of the methodology is explored.

Any bill of final demand can be analyzed by computer methodology. Thus, the opportunity to analyze the resource costs and regional impact of other types of public or private projects depends only on the development of their detailed final demands. Moreover, while the present analysis relates to the 1960 economy, with its national and regional patterns of unutilized labor and capital resources, an analysis easily could be conducted for different time periods with either more or less unused capacity. A third dimension that could be explored further is that of regional impact. The choice of regions for analysis is essentially openended. A fourth dimension might be the sensitivity of conclusions to the assumptions built into each of the models.

The computer methodology is preserved in a set of ten Fortran programs written for the Control Data Corporation 3600. The programs can be run as an integrated set with the output of one program written on magnetic tape as input to the next. The total computational time for a single bill of final demands is roughly two minutes for the complete national and regional analysis. The programs are described briefly below in nontechnical language to provide understanding of the capacity of the computer methodology and the information content of each program. The computer methodology is further explained in the flow chart shown in Figure 6A–1, on page 124.

THE NATIONAL MODEL

PROG 0   —*Calculation of National Gross Output*

Card input   —the bill of final demand for materials, equipment and supplies for any expenditure by 82 industries

Tape input	—the 1958 U.S. Department of Commerce, Office of Business Economics inverse input-output matrix (82×82)
Calculation	—for each bill of final demand the gross output generated by 82 industries, calculated by matrix multiplication
Printer output	—the bill of final demand and the gross output, printed out for 82 industries
Tape output	—the bill of final demand and gross output by 82 industries written on tape

PROG 1	—*Calculation of Man-hours of Off-site Employment for 137 Industries*
Card input	—conversion factors for gross output in dollars to man-hours for 82 industries —percentages of man-hours by 61 industries that may be attributed to 137 industries (this may differ according to project type)[1]
Tape input	—the tape output of **PROG** 0; the bill of final demand and gross output for 82 industries
Calculations	—for each bill of final demand: • gross output segregated into the original final demand for materials, equipment, and supplies and the remaining indirect industrial components • dollar output values converted to labor man-hour requirements for the two components above • 82 industries are collapsed into 61 sectors for the two components • 61 industries are expanded into 137 sectors using the appropriate percentage conversion figures for the two components[1]
Printer output	—all of the calculations described above may be printed out in full detail
Tape output	—for each final demand vector: total man-hours by 137 industries

PROG 2	—*Calculation of Off-site Labor Cost by Occupation*
Card input	—average annual incomes for 156 occupations —percentage labor share of gross output by 82 industries

---

[1] See footnote 21, Chapter II.

Tape input   —conversion matrix (137 × 156) percentages of man-hours of 137 industries attributable to 156 occupations
       —output of PROG 0, gross output by 82 industries
       —output of PROG 1, man-hours by 137 industries

Calculations   —for each final-demand vector:
       • man-hours by 137 industries converted to man-hours by 156 occupations by matrix multiplication
       • off-site labor cost by 156 occupations calculated and totaled from man-hours and average annual incomes by occupation
       • total off-site labor cost calculated by a second method applying labor shares by 82 industries to the gross output data of PROG 0
       • off-site labor costs by 156 occupations multiplied by a constant so that their total will equal the total of the 82-sector calculation[2]

Printer output   —all of the calculations described above may be printed out in full detail

Tape output   —For each final demand vector:
       • man-hours by 156 occupations
       • adjusted off-site labor costs by 156 occupations

PROG 3   *—Calculation of Total Labor Cost and Shadow Labor Cost by Occupation*

Card input   —on-site labor costs by occupation for each final demand vector
       —unemployment rates by occupation
       —shadow labor factors by occupation[3]

Tape input   —output of PROG 2, man-hours by occupation, and labor cost by occupation

Calculations   —for each final demand vector:
       • off-site labor cost generated by the bill of final demand (calculated in PROG 2) added to on-site labor costs for 156 occupations

---

[2] The 82-industry calculation was considered a more reliable measure of total labor cost. The adjustment constants ranged from .97 to 1.14 for the projects in the analysis.

[3] Shadow factors are percentages to be applied to the labor cost by occupation to assess what portion of cost represents a diversion of resources from some other use. The remainder of this labor demand is met by resources otherwise unemployed. Shadow labor factors for the study were calculated from a set of functions relating the shadow factor to occupational unemployment rates. See Chapter IV, the section on expected labor and capital response functions.

- shadow labor cost by occupation calculated by multiplying the occupational labor cost figures by the appropriate shadow labor factors
- a weighted index of the rate of unemployed off-site labor utilization calculated by multiplying the unemployment rate by off-site labor man-hours for each occupation
- a weighted index of the rate of unemployed total labor utilization calculated by multiplying the unemployment rate by total labor cost for each occupation

Printer output   —total labor cost and 156-occupation breakdown
—9 summary occupations for the total cost by dollars and as a per cent of total
—total shadow labor cost and 156-occupation breakdown
—9 summary occupations for total shadow cost by dollars and as a per cent of total
—the two indices of unemployment described above

PROG 4   —*Calculation of Capital Cost and Other Value-Added Components*

Card input   —ratios of net interest, capital consumption allowance, indirect business taxes, corporate profits, proprietor and rental income, and employee compensation to gross output for 82 industries
—rates of capacity utilization for 82 industries
—shadow capital factors for 82 industries[4]

Tape input   —output of PROG 0, gross output by 82 industries

Calculations   —for each final-demand vector:
- 6 sets of ratios described above multiplied by gross output by 82 industries to compute total components of net interest, capital consumption allowance, indirect business taxes, corporate profits, proprietor and rental income, and employee compensation
- partial capital income for each sector (sum of net interest and corporate profits) multiplied by the shadow capital factor to calculate shadow capital cost by industry; capital consumption allowance added at full value

---

[4] Shadow capital factors similar in concept to the shadow labor factors are calculated from a set of functions relating the shadow factor to the rate of capital utilization by industry. See Chapter IV, the section cited above in footnote 3.

- a weighted index of the rate of unemployed capital utilization calculated by multiplying the utilization rate by capital income for each sector

Printout — all of the calculations described above are printed out

THE REGIONAL MODEL

PROG 5 — *Calculation of Appropriate Regional Input-Output Matrices as First Step to Regional Analysis*

Card input — control cards delineating which of the industries are to be Local industries and which are to be national industries [5]
— input-output coefficients of the 1958 Office of Business Economics study (82×82)

Calculations — coefficients of the 82×82 matrix are segregated into two matrices: $d \times d$ (Local industries to Local industries) and $d \times q$ (Local industries to national industries)
— the $d \times d$ matrix is subtracted from I, the identity matrix, and inverted to produce an inverse input-output matrix for Local industries

Printout — all calculations printed out

Tape output — the $d \times q$ matrix and the inverted $d \times d$ matrix

PROG 6 — *Regional Distribution of Gross Output for Project Construction Assumed to be Located in Each of S Regions*

Card input — control cards delineating which of the industries are to be Local industries and which are to be national industries
— control card for national industries indicating what regional preference function should be applied to distribute gross output among the regions
— regional distribution coefficients for each national industry for each of 10 regions of the United States

---

[5] Local industries are those which meet the project requirements completely from within the region in which the final demand is imposed. National industries satisfy project requirements nationally with the split between project region and rest of the nation expressed as a function of the regional distribution of national industry capacity.

Tape input   —output of PROG 0, final demand and gross output by 82 industries

—output of PROG 5, $d \times q$ and $d \times d$ input-output coefficients

Calculations[6]   —per cent of national industry final demand supplied within the region in which the project is assumed to be constructed, calculated by multiplying the regional distribution coefficients by the appropriate regional preference function parameter specified by control card[7]

—for each final-demand vector for each region in which the project is assumed to be constructed:

—I: portion of national industry final demand purchased in the region in which project is assumed to be located calculated on the basis of percentages described above

—II: remaining portion of final demand and remaining portion of gross output for national industries distributed regionally according to regional distribution coefficients

—III: Parts I and II of national industry final demand and gross output by region consolidated

—IV: Local industry output requirements caused by transactions with national industry calculated region by region by multiplying the national gross output in each region (III) by the Local-to-national industry transaction matrix calculated in PROG 5

—V: the above Local industry output requirements by region (IV) consolidated with the final project demands for Local industry goods attributed to the region in which the project is assumed to be located

—VI: the total "final" output requirements for Local industries (V) multiplied by the Local-to-Local inverse input-output matrix to calculate the gross output of Local industries by region

Printout   —total gross output by region with 17 industrial summary sectors printed out and percentages of each

[6] The calculations of PROG 6 are more easily understood in matrix algebra form in Appendix 4 and Appendix 5.

[7] For example, industry 5 has .106 of national industry capacity in region II. By assumption, the appropriate regional preference function parameter is 2. Thus, region II produces $2 \times .106 = .212$ of the final demand for industry 5 if the project is located in region II. The remainder of the gross output, including .788 of final demand, is distributed nationally according to the regional distribution coefficients.

region to the national total printed in an $18 \times 10 \times 2$ array (for each final-demand vector, there are 10 of the above arrays as the project is assumed to be located in each of the 10 regions)

Tape output —the full industry detail for final demand and gross output for each of the 10 regions written on tape corresponding to each printout above, each tape record consisting of an $82 \times 10 \times 2$ array

The following PROG 1: Regional, PROG 2: Regional, and PROG 3: Regional accomplish the same analysis as the national analysis described above in PROG 1, PROG 2, and PROG 3. The computations are done for each regional vector (10), for each assumed project location (10), thus effectively multiplying the previous computational task by a factor of 100. The descriptions of these three programs will only enumerate the differences from the national analysis.

PROG 1: *Regional*

Tape Input —tape output of PROG 6 (rather than PROG 0), direct demands and gross output by 82 industries and 10 regions

Printout —limited to the 137×10 array of man-hours by region and by industry

Tape Output —for each final-demand vector and for each assumed project location, the 137×10 array described above written on tape

PROG 2: *Regional*

Tape input —tape output of PROG 1: Regional, man-hours by 137 industries and 10 regions

Printout —for each final-demand vector, and for each assumed project location, the adjusted labor cost by occupation printed out for 19 summary occupations for each region (19×10 array); the row value as a per cent of the national row total also printed

Tape output —the full occupational detail (156×10 array) written on tape for each table described above

PROG 3: *Regional*

Card input —unemployment rates for 156 occupations and 10 regions

	—unemployment rates for 156 occupations and 10 states (one state for each region in which the project is assumed to be located)
Tape input	—tape output of PROG 2: Regional, labor cost by 156 occupations and 10 regions
Calculations	—different from PROG 3 in that shadow labor ratios by occupation and region are calculated as functions of the appropriate unemployment rate by the program (rather than read as input data)
	—a second shadow labor ratio by occupation and region calculated from state unemployment rates (this set of ratios applied to the on-site labor costs by occupation)
Printout	—For each final-demand vector, for each assumption of project location:
	• total labor costs, shadow labor cost, and shadow as per cent of total costs shown for the 10 regions first excluding on-site labor costs, then including on-site costs
	• only a single index of unemployment calculated, weighted by total labor costs

FURTHER USES OF THE PROGRAM

These programs make it possible to analyze the impact of any final-demand vector assumed to be imposed on any region in 1960, describing gross output, labor demand in man-hours, labor cost, unemployed labor demand, capital demand, unemployed capital demand, regional distribution of gross output by industry, and regional distribution of labor cost or man-hours by occupation. The data input needed comprises the requirements of a project broken down into materials, equipment, and supplies by 82 industries and on-site labor costs by 156 occupations. This same procedure was followed assuming a final-demand vector equivalent to GNP final demand in distribution and another equivalent to national personal consumption expenditure demand. These runs served to illuminate the special nature of investment in water resource projects in contrast to the more general pattern of final demands in the U.S. economy.

To analyze the impact of any regional investment project at another point of time, it is necessary to develop, at a minimum, unemployment rates for 156 occupations for the analysis of PROG 3, unutilized industrial capacity for 82 industrial sectors for the analysis of PROG 4, and unemployment rates for 156 occupations and 10 regions for the analysis of PROG 3: Regional.

Other time-dependent parameters, which may be varied depending upon their availability, are the input-output coefficients of PROG 0 and PROG 5, the dollar value to man-hour conversion ratios of PROG 1 and PROG 1: Regional, and the average labor incomes by occupation, labor shares of gross national product by industry, and the industry-to-occupation conversion ratios of PROG 2 and PROG 2: Regional.

In another mode of experimentation with the model, the United States may be carved into a different set of regions to be analyzed. The changes in data would be the regional distribution coefficients, the regional preference functions of PROG 6, and the unemployment rates by occupation and region of PROG 3: Regional.

Differing assumptions as to relationships of shadow labor cost to unemployment may be tested by changing the shadow labor factors by occupation read in PROG 3. Similar experimentation may be made in PROG 4 with respect to shadow capital cost and the measure of capital utilization.

Similarly, experiments on the regional distribution of gross output and labor cost can be made by varying the assumptions about the set of national and Local industries in PROG 5 and PROG 6, and the functions to distribute gross output by industry among the regions of PROG 6.

FIGURE 6A–1. FLOW CHART ILLUSTRATING COMPUTER METHODOLOGY FOR SECTORAL DEMAND AND SHADOW COST MODELS

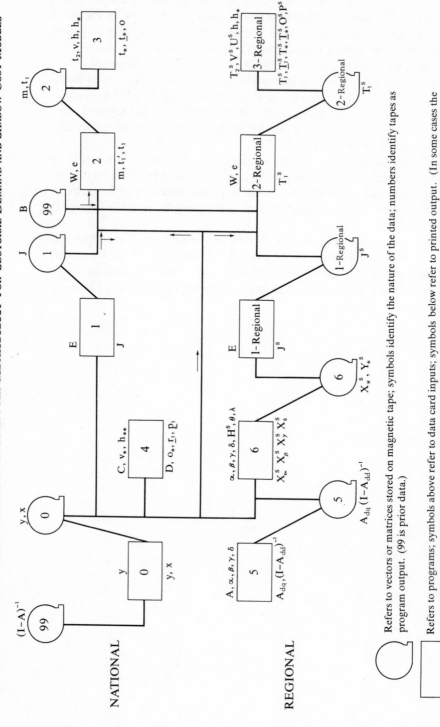

Refers to vectors or matrices stored on magnetic tape; symbols identify the nature of the data; numbers identify tapes as program output. (99 is prior data.)

Refers to programs; symbols above refer to data card inputs; symbols below refer to printed output. (In some cases the matrix is condensed, totaled, or percentages are calculated.)

APPENDIX 7
REGIONAL DISTRIBUTION COEFFICIENTS

Table 7A–1. Input-Output Sectors and the Regional Distribution Coefficients for the National Industries

Input-output numbers and industry categories	Industry type[a]	I New England	II Mid-Atlantic	III East North Central	IV West North Central	V Southeast	VI Lower Atlantic	VII Kentucky-Tennessee	VIII West South Central	IX Mountain	X West Coast
1 Livestock & products	C	.027	.073	.212	.309	.082	.032	.030	.085	.072	.077
2 Other agriculture	C	.016	.037	.133	.203	.155	.023	.033	.164	.075	.163
3 Forestry & fisheries	C	.182	.053	.018	.006	.171	.121	.004	.156	.006	.286
4 Agricultural services	C	.083	.196	.157	.080	.094	.052	.024	.065	.036	.213
5 Iron ore mining	B	—	.106	.106	.529	.062	.010	.024	.024	.115	.024
6 Nonferrous metal mining	B	—	.040	.104	.044	.017	—	.017	.030	.718	.030
7 Coal mining	B	.001	.279	.143	.010	.036	.365	.132	.006	.029	.001
8 Crude petroleum & natural gas	B	—	.018	.044	.046	.015	.011	.010	.683	.084	.090
9 Stone & clay mining	L	.035	.092	.269	.117	.132	.057	.045	.077	.060	.115
10 Chemical & fertilizer mining	B	.009	.019	.065	.019	.148	.019	.046	.259	.269	.148
11 New construction	X	—	—	—	—	—	—	—	—	—	—
12 Maintenance construction	L	—	—	—	—	—	—	—	—	—	—
13 Ordnance & accessories	B	.075	.183	.100	.068	.026	.044	.013	.014	.074	.405
14 Food & kindred products	C	.047	.202	.246	.137	.068	.043	.032	.067	.028	.129
15 Tobacco manufactures	C	.008	.158	.017	—	.468	.190	.159	—	—	*
16 Fabrics, yarn	B	.177	.141	.010	.001	.588	.048	.019	.012	—	.004
17 Rugs, miscellaneous textiles	B	.207	.285	.154	.013	.214	.056	.020	.013	—	.036
18 Apparel	B	.070	.515	.073	.034	.139	.040	.046	.031	.003	.048
19 Miscellaneous fabricated textiles	B	.076	.428	.189	.048	.089	.034	.020	.031	.004	.082
20 Lumber & wood products	B	.049	.060	.106	.039	.139	.041	.030	.076	.060	.399
21 Wooden containers	B	.069	.098	.172	.035	.230	.065	.085	.065	.003	.178
22 Household furniture	C	.060	.185	.240	.034	.192	.061	.055	.050	.007	.117
23 Other furniture	C	.040	.265	.391	.053	.050	.045	.008	.041	.012	.095
24 Paper & allied products	C	.145	.203	.253	.043	.139	.035	.019	.070	.001	.090
25 Paperboard containers	C	.087	.302	.294	.062	.065	.042	.016	.037	.004	.091
26 Printing & publishing	L	—	—	—	—	—	—	—	—	—	—
27 Chemicals	C	.026	.224	.203	.051	.070	.109	.066	.159	.018	.073
28 Plastics & synthetics	C	.050	.186	.109	.015	.149	.234	.181	.064	.012	.012
29 Drugs	C	.048	.408	.326	.064	.034	.035	.011	.010	.001	.062
30 Paints & allied products	C	.036	.288	.363	.066	.038	.023	.033	.037	.006	.109
31 Petroleum products	B	.012	.176	.202	.046	.010	.010	.006	.377	.034	.128
32 Rubber & plastics	B	.164	.187	.426	.034	.029	.033	.014	.021	.020	.072
33 Leather tanning	C	.302	.297	.264	.016	.044	.044	.005	.005	—	.022
34 Footwear & other leather products	C	.325	.294	.147	.107	.016	.024	.040	.018	.010	.021
35 Glass & glass products	C	.009	.382	.313	.002	.066	.113	.012	.031	—	.071
36 Stone & clay products	C	.055	.210	.271	.089	.080	.054	.033	.075	.032	.103
37 Iron & steel	C	.025	.317	.418	.033	.045	.066	.013	.020	.024	.040
38 Nonferrous metals	C	.108	.234	.276	.025	.012	.044	.002	.053	.145	.099
39 Metal containers	C	.014	.252	.328	.061	.056	.053	—	.078	.006	.151

No.	Type[a]	Industry										
40	C	Heating & plumbing products	.038	.259	.302	.070	.064	.040	.030	.061	.019	.117
41	C	Screw machine products	.109	.233	.516	.029	.019	.017	.008	.006	.001	.063
42	C	Other fabricated metal products	.138	.223	.422	.041	.011	.017	.029	.027	.004	.088
43	B	Engines & turbines	.101	.355	.459	.029	.005	.011	.011	.002	—	.027
44	A	Farm machinery	.002	.062	.530	.270	.020	.005	.058	.013	.005	.033
45	B	Construction & mining machinery	.012	.081	.534	.073	.016	.012	.007	.174	.025	.068
46	C	Materials handling machinery	.030	.279	.443	.052	.023	.007	.023	.043	.010	.092
47	A	Metalworking machinery	.151	.170	.580	.025	.009	.011	.005	.004	.002	.043
48	C	Special industry machinery	.196	.279	.307	.029	.056	.032	.013	.023	.002	.063
49	C	General industrial machinery	.143	.271	.430	.028	.010	.010	.008	.022	.006	.073
50	C	Machine shop products	.078	.183	.365	.063	.035	.023	.021	.047	.014	.172
51	B	Office machines	.106	.394	.303	.067	.001	.004	.003	.003	.016	.103
52	B	Service industry machines	.069	.267	.363	.128	.026	.010	.022	.041	.012	.063
53	B	Electric industrial equipment	.084	.301	.422	.052	.022	.020	.005	.009	.004	.081
54	B	Household appliances	.091	.211	.465	.053	.010	.019	.076	.005	*	.070
55	B	Electric lighting equipment	.091	.211	.465	.053	.010	.019	.076	.005	*	.070
56	B	Communication equipment	.110	.369	.288	.029	.032	.034	.009	.019	.008	.103
57	B	Electronic components	.110	.369	.288	.029	.032	.034	.009	.019	.008	.103
58	A	Miscellaneous electrical machinery	.084	.301	.422	.052	.022	.020	.005	.009	.004	.081
59	A	Motor vehicles	.009	.120	.726	.041	.022	.017	.009	.012	.001	.044
60	B	Aircraft	.082	.125	.147	.094	.034	.035	.009	.076	.011	.394
61	C	Other transportation equipment	.132	.222	.188	.028	.102	.136	.009	.067	.003	.114
62	C	Scientific instruments	.128	.494	.208	.058	.005	.013	.008	.017	.004	.067
63	C	Optical & photographic equipment	.128	.494	.208	.058	.005	.013	.008	.017	.004	.067
64	C	Miscellaneous manufacturing	.181	.370	.235	.044	.058	.003	.014	.014	.019	.061
65	L	Transportation & warehousing	— —	— —	— —	— —	— —	— —	— —	— —	— —	— —
66	L	Communications, except radio & TV	— —	— —	— —	— —	— —	— —	— —	— —	— —	— —
67	L	Radio & TV broadcasting	— —	— —	— —	— —	— —	— —	— —	— —	— —	— —
68	L	Electricity, gas, water, sanitary services	— —	— —	— —	— —	— —	— —	— —	— —	— —	— —
69	L	Wholesale & retail trade	— —	— —	— —	— —	— —	— —	— —	— —	— —	— —
70	L	Finance & insurance	— —	— —	— —	— —	— —	— —	— —	— —	— —	— —
71	L	Real estate & rental	— —	— —	— —	— —	— —	— —	— —	— —	— —	— —
72	C	Personal & repair services	.052	.167	.152	.028	.033	.164	.062	.030	.030	.284
73	L	Business services	— —	— —	— —	— —	— —	— —	— —	— —	— —	— —
74	L	Research & development	— —	— —	— —	— —	— —	— —	— —	— —	— —	— —
75	L	Automobile repair services	— —	— —	— —	— —	— —	— —	— —	— —	— —	— —
76	L	Amusements	— —	— —	— —	— —	— —	— —	— —	— —	— —	— —
77	L	Medical & educational services	— —	— —	— —	— —	— —	— —	— —	— —	— —	— —
78	L	Federal government enterprise	— —	— —	— —	— —	— —	— —	— —	— —	— —	— —
79	L	State & local government enterprises	— —	— —	— —	— —	— —	— —	— —	— —	— —	— —
80	X	Imports	— —	— —	— —	— —	— —	— —	— —	— —	— —	— —
81	L	Business travel, entertainment	— —	— —	— —	— —	— —	— —	— —	— —	— —	— —
82	L	Office supplies	— —	— —	— —	— —	— —	— —	— —	— —	— —	— —

Asterisk (*) means less than .0005 but greater than zero; dash (—) means zero; double dashes (– –) across rows for industry types L and X mean regional distribution coefficients are not used.

[a] A in this column refers to Type A industries, defined as those which produce for a truly national market. B and C signify Type B and Type C industries which serve neither completely national nor completely local markets. L stands for Local industries, those which produce within a region and supply only the demands of local buyers. X indicates those industries whose output is not regionally allocable.

THE ESTIMATION OF EXCESS INDUSTRIAL
CAPACITY IN 1960

IN RECENT YEARS, several concepts of capacity utilization—each with its own developed methodology—have been proposed for the estimation of excess industrial capacity. Each of these approaches is based on a different concept of capacity and a different estimation technique. Consequently, consistency among the estimates is seldom achieved. The four measures which we use in forming the combined capacity utilization rate estimates are those prepared by (1) the Economics Research Unit at the Wharton School of Finance and Commerce, (2) the McGraw-Hill Company's Department of Economics, (3) the National Industrial Conference Board, and (4) Bert G. Hickman.[1]

In the Wharton School measure, trend lines constructed through peaks of industrial output are assumed to represent that output which would have been forthcoming if all resources had been utilized. The ratio of actual output to the trend forms the measure of capacity utilization.[2] While the Wharton School measure uses peak output as a bench mark, the method employed by the National Industrial Conference Board uses a minimum capital-output ratio. Assuming that capacity is fully utilized in the year of the minimum ratio, increases in the ratio demonstrate excess capacity. The measure of excess capacity is the ratio of the minimum capital-output ratio to each year's observed ratio. The McGraw-Hill and Hickman measures use techniques quite different from these bench-mark comparisons. The McGraw-Hill estimates are formulated from responses to the annual survey of plant and equipment in which replies to questionnaires are received from firms representing about 40 per cent of total manufacturing employment. Hickman's estimates are

---

[1] Daniel Creamer, *Capital Expansion and Capacity in Post-War Manufacturing*, Studies in Business Economics, No. 72 (New York: National Industrial Conference Board, 1961); Creamer and Delos R. Smith, *Recent Changes in Manufacturing Capacity, Studies in Business Economics*, No. 79 (New York: National Industrial Conference Board, 1962); Bert G. Hickman, *Investment Demand and U.S. Economic Growth* (Washington: Brookings Institution, 1965); Joint Economic Committee, *Measures of Productive Capacity*, Hearings before the Subcommittee on Economic Statistics, 87 Cong. 2 sess. (1962); and Economics Research Unit, Department of Economics, Wharton School of Finance and Commerce, University of Pennsylvania.

[2] We are indebted to Lawrence M. Klein and Robert Summers of the Economics Research Unit for the Wharton School estimates in 30-industry detail.

based on the relationship of actual output to statistically derived estimates of capital stock and, hence, optimum or capacity output.

In Figure 8A–1, the estimated rates of excess capacity in 1960 for
each of thirty-one industries are presented for each of the four estimating
techniques described.[3] Because of limited coverage of some of the
indexes, a number of the industries have fewer than four estimates.

In the case of both the Wharton School and the Conference Board
estimates, a rate of capacity utilization of 100 is taken to be full employment of capital resources. This is justified in that the capacity estimates
of both of these methods presume to measure utilization as a percentage
of economic capacity. For the McGraw-Hill index, an operating rate of
92 per cent is assumed to be full utilization. The replies of respondents
have often cited this rate to be the "preferred operating rate," as opposed
to the 100 per cent figure which is generally taken to mean maximum
output under normal work schedules irrespective of the level of marginal
cost. In the case of Hickman's index, we have adopted the following procedure: Because the design of the Hickman index is such as to permit
observed utilization rates to range substantially over 100 per cent, the
highest utilization rate observed in an industry in the decade prior to
1960 was taken to be full utilization, and the observed utilization rate in
1960 was expressed as a percentage of this bench-mark figure. Implicit
in this procedure are the assumptions (1) that the highest observed
utilization rate in the 1950–60 period represents that rate at which
capacity output is achieved and (2) that the industry cost structure
remains virtually unchanged over the decade. This last assumption
involves the requirement that the ratio of output at peak capacity (the
level of output at which marginal costs begin to rise rapidly) and output
at economic capacity (the level of output at minimum average cost)
remains secularly constant within an industry.

Finally, it should be noted that both the Conference Board index and
the McGraw-Hill index had to be adjusted to place them on a comparative analytic basis. As published, the McGraw-Hill capacity-utilization
percentage relates to the end of each year; the December output at an
annual rate as a percentage of end-of-year capacity. To transform this
to an average utilization rate for the entire year, the published industry
rates are multiplied by the ratio of average monthly production for the
year in question to December production in that year.[4] The Conference
Board yearly estimates refer to operating rates during the peak quarter
of a year. These indexes were adjusted to an average annual basis by
multiplying the published industry indexes by the ratio of average

---

[3] The input-output numbers of industries corresponding to the industries listed in
Figure 8A–1 are stated in parenthesis behind the thirty-one industry titles.
[4] The 1959 revised Federal Reserve Board production indexes were used for this
adjustment.

FIGURE 8A-1. MEASURES OF EXCESS CAPACITY: COMPARISON OF ESTIMATES FOR 1960

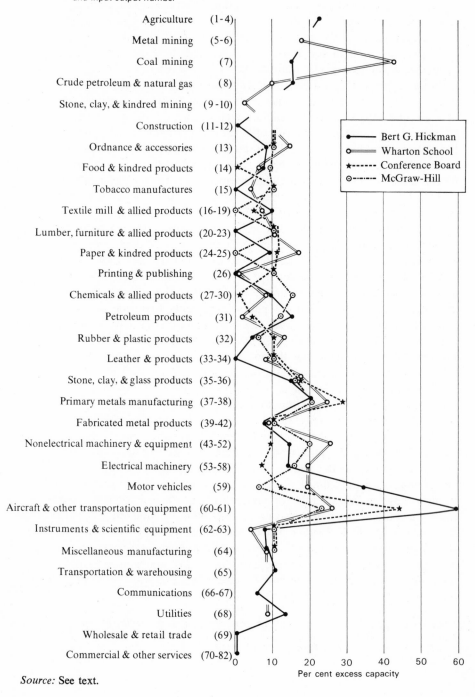

Source: See text.

annual production on a quarterly basis for the year in question to peak quarterly production in that year.[5]

As can be seen in Figure 8A–1, there exists a substantial lack of agreement among the indexes on the extent of excess capacity in a number of industries. For other industries, the four estimates nearly coincide. More important, all of the indexes succeed in pointing out those industries with very low levels of excess capacity (textiles, lumber and furniture) and very high levels (primary metals manufacturing, non-electrical machinery and equipment, transportation equipment). In our analysis of shadow cost estimation, the level of excess capacity employed is that defined by the arithmetic mean of the two interior estimates for each industry.

[5] See also Hickman, *op. cit.*, pp. 112–20; Creamer, *op. cit.*, Appendix F; and Almarin Phillips, "Industrial Capacity, An Appraisal of Measures of Capacity," *American Economic Review, Papers and Proceedings,* Vol. 53 (May 1963), pp. 275–92, for a further comparison of these measures of capacity utilization.

MATHEMATICAL FORMULATION OF THE NATIONAL AND REGIONAL SOCIAL COST ESTIMATION MODELS

ESTIMATION OF THE SOCIAL COST of project inputs requires the detailed disaggregation of the factor input demands and the linking of this information to the degree of unused productive capacity for the particular factor at the same level of disaggregation. This analysis is made in the national model for the primary factors—labor and capital—presuming that national rates of unused productive capacity hold for the factors employed. Factors other than labor and capital are presumed to have the same ratio of social cost to money cost as the sum of the two primary factors.

The regional model carries the analysis a step further in recognition that rates of unused productive capacity for labor vary among regions. Consequently, as the project is assumed to be located in different regions of the country the social cost will vary with the changes in labor demand by region.

The conventions of notational use are similar to Appendices 1 and 4. There are N industries, Z occupations, and S regions. All other capital letters represent matrices, lower case letters represent vectors or scalars, and Greek letters represent scalars. The hat symbol ^ represents a matrix of the same dimensionality as the vector under the symbol where the elements of the vector have been superimposed on the principal diagonal of a null matrix. The use of a line under a symbol (for example, $\underline{r}_1$) indicates the social cost of the elements of the vector or matrix as contrasted with the money cost. The symbol $'$ indicates the transpose of a vector, the symbol $^{-1}$ the inverse of a matrix. The symbol u represents a row vector whose components are all ones.

NOTATIONAL GLOSSARY

The following symbols from the national model are carried over from Appendix 1. They are named below and the equation where they are derived is shown. (For more complete information see Appendix 1.)

r_1—net interest by industry.	Equation 6
c_1—capital consumption allowance by industry.	Equation 6
p_1—corporate profits by industry.	Equation 6

t_*—labor cost by occupation.   Equation 8

f—total cost for project construction.   Given

The following symbols from the regional model are carried over from Appendix 4, which provides more complete definition and derivation.

T_1^S—off-site labor cost by occupation and region.   Equation 14

T_2^S—on-site labor cost by occupation and region.   Given

T_*^S—total labor cost by occupation and region.   Equation 15

The following symbols are introduced in this appendix:

h—column vector $(Z \times 1)$ of the assumed base unemployment rate by occupation below which the shadow cost and money cost are presumed equal.

H—rectangular matrix $(Z \times S)$ of the h column vector repeated S times.

h_*—scalar, the assumed unemployment rate for all occupations above which the shadow cost of labor is presumed to be zero.

h_{**}—scalar, the assumed rate of unutilized capacity for all industries above which the shadow cost of capital is presumed to be zero.[1]

$[1]$—column vector or rectangular matrix of all ones of appropriate dimensionality.

v—column vector $(Z \times 1)$ of national unemployment rates by occupation.

v_*—column vector $(N \times 1)$ of national rates of unutilized capital by industry.

V^S—rectangular matrix $(Z \times S)$ of unemployment rates each column of which shows unemployment rates for a particular region by occupation.

U^S—rectangular matrix $(Z \times S)$ of unemployment rates each column of which shows unemployment rates for a particular state within the region by occupation.

o—column vector $(Z \times 1)$ of national shadow factors for labor by occupation.

o_*—column vector $(N \times 1)$ of national shadow factors for capital by industry.

---

[1] The elements of h, h_*, and h_{**} are the necessary parameters to calculate the synthetic labor response function and the synthetic capital response function described in Chapter 4. The particular function then gives the probability that the resource demand is met from the idle pool of resources. The relevant range of the function for a particular occupation, z, is then h_z to h_* for the unemployment rate, the probability ranges from zero to one, and the shadow factor inversely from one to zero. The relevant range of the function for capital for all industrial sectors is from zero to h_{**} for the rate of unutilized capacity. The response function equations are shown in equations 1, 3, 7, and 8 of this appendix.

O^S—rectangular matrix ($Z \times S$) of regional shadow factors each column of which shows labor shadow factors for a particular region by occupation.

P^S—rectangular matrix ($Z \times S$) of regional shadow factors each column of which shows labor shadow factors for a particular state by occupation.

Δ—scalar, total social cost of the contract expenditure.

η—scalar, weighted average of unemployed labor resources used by the project.

σ—scalar, total shadow labor cost in the regional model.

NATIONAL SOCIAL COST ESTIMATION MODEL

Labor shadow factors for each occupation are calculated by the assumed synthetic response functions of the national unemployment rates by occupation.

$$o = [1] - .5\left[\sin\left\{ \pi(h_*[1] - h)^{-1}(v - h) - \frac{\pi}{2}[1]\right\} + [1]\right]. \qquad (1)[2]$$

[2] The sine of the $Z \times 1$ vector in brackets implies the sine of each one of the elements. The diagonal matrix ($h_*[1] - h$) has the following elements:

$$\begin{bmatrix} h_* - h_1 & 0 & 0 \ldots \ldots 0 \\ 0 & h_* - h_2 & 0 \ldots \ldots 0 \\ 0 & 0 & h_* - h_3 \ldots 0 \\ \cdot & \cdot & \cdot \quad \cdot \\ \cdot & \cdot & \cdot \quad \cdot \\ \cdot & \cdot & \cdot \quad \cdot \\ 0 & 0 & 0 \ldots h_* - h_z \end{bmatrix}$$

The inverse of this matrix ($h_*[1] - h)^{-1}$ has the following elements:

$$\begin{bmatrix} \dfrac{1}{h_* - h_1} & 0 & 0 \ldots \ldots \ldots \ldots 0 \\ 0 & \dfrac{1}{h_* - h_2} & \ldots 0 \ldots \ldots \ldots \ldots 0 \\ 0 & 0 & \dfrac{1}{h_* - h_3} \ldots \ldots \ldots \ldots 0 \\ \cdot & \cdot & \cdot \qquad \cdot \\ \cdot & \cdot & \cdot \qquad \cdot \\ 0 & 0 & 0 \ldots \ldots \ldots \dfrac{1}{h_* - h_z} \end{bmatrix}$$

The implied equation for each element of o is as follows

$$o_z = 1 - .5\left[\sin\left\{\pi\left(\frac{v_z - h_z}{h_* - h_z}\right) - \frac{\pi}{2}\right\} + 1\right].\qquad(1a)[3]$$

(v_z is replaced by h_z if $v_z < h_z$; v_z is replaced by h_* if $v_z > h_*$).

Two other response functions were utilized in the model to signify the upper and lower bounds for the shadow factors. The lower-bound shadow cost response function for a single sector is

$$o_z = 1 - \sin\left\{\frac{\pi}{2}\left(\frac{v_z - h_z}{h_* - h_z}\right)\right\}.\qquad(1b)$$

The upper-bound social cost model for a single sector is

$$o_z = 1 - \sin\left\{\pi/2 - \frac{\pi}{2}\left[\frac{v_z - h_z}{h_* - h_z}\right]\right\}.\qquad(1c)$$

Shadow labor cost by occupation is then calculated by multiplying total labor cost by occupation by the respective shadow factors.

$$t_* = \hat{o}\, t_*.\qquad(2)$$

Capital shadow factors for each industry are calculated from synthetic functions of the national rate of unutilized capacity by industry.

$$o_* = [1] - .5\left[\sin\left\{\left(\pi\frac{1}{h_{**}}v_*\right) - \frac{\pi}{2}[1]\right\} + [1]\right].\qquad(3)[4]$$

Alternative formulations for the capital response function are analogous to ($1b$) and ($1c$) above.

Shadow capital cost by industry is then calculated by multiplying net

---

[3] This equation may be better understood through a numerical example for a particular occupational sector, for example, salesworkers. For salesworkers the base unemployment rate, h_z, is .021, and $h_* = .25$ for all occupations. Assuming an unemployment rate of .06 for salesworkers ($v_z = .06$),

$$\frac{v_z - h_z}{h_* - h_z} = \frac{.060 - .021}{.250 - .021} = .170.$$

This fraction varies from 0 to 1 as the unemployment rate for salesworkers varies from .021 to .25. This fraction is converted to radians by multiplying by π and subtracting $\pi/2$. The angle thus varies from $-\pi/2$ to $+\pi/2$ over the range of unemployment rates. The sine varies accordingly from -1 to $+1$ over this same range. Adding 1 to the sine converts the range from zero to $+2$ and multiplying by .5 converts this function to a probability measure varying between zero and $+1$. In our example, for .06 unemployment, the angle in radians becomes

$$3.1416\,(.170) - 1.5708 = -1.0367.$$

The sine of the above angle is $-.86$. The sine is converted to probability measure:

$$.5\,(-.86 + 1) = .07.$$

The shadow factor is then:

$$1 - .07 = .93.$$

[4] This is the same functional form as equation 1 where h_{**} is substituted for h_*, v_* for v, and the null vector is substituted for h.

interest plus corporate profits by industry by their respective shadow factors and adding capital consumption allowances by industry at full value.

$$(\underline{r_1} + \underline{p_1} + \underline{c_1}) = \hat{o}_* \, (r_1 + p_1) + c_1. \tag{4}$$

The ratio of social cost to money cost for the traceable labor and capital is multiplied by the total contract cost to provide the social cost of the total expenditure.

$$\Delta = \left(\frac{u \, t_* + u(\underline{r_1} + \underline{p_1} + \underline{c_1})}{u \, t_* + u(r_1 + p_1 + c_1)} \right) \cdot f. \tag{5}$$

A weighted average of the fraction of unemployed labor resources utilized by the project is derived by weighting national unemployment rates (by occupation) by the labor cost attributed to that occupation.

$$\eta = \frac{v' t_*}{u \, t_*} \tag{6}$$

REGIONAL SOCIAL COST ESTIMATION MODEL

In this model, shadow labor factors by occupation are derived for each of S regions by the same synthetic labor response functions as in the national model.

Regional unemployment rates by occupation provide the input to the synthetic functions required to compute shadow factors for off-site labor.

$$O^S = [1] - .5 \left[\sin \left\{ \pi(h_*[1] - h)^{-1} (V^S - H) - \frac{\pi}{2} [1] \right\} + [1] \right]. \tag{7}$$

State unemployment rates by occupation provide the input to the synthetic functions required to compute shadow factors for on-site labor.

$$P^S = [1] - .5 \left[\sin \left\{ \pi(h_*[1] - h)^{-1} (U^S - H) - \frac{\pi}{2} [1] \right\} + [1] \right]. \tag{8}$$

Equations 7 and 8 differ from equation 1 only in that a rectangular matrix $(Z \times S)$ of regional unemployment rates is substituted for the $(Z \times 1)$ vector of national unemployment rates, and a rectangular matrix $(Z \times S)$ of shadow factors is derived.

Shadow off-site labor cost by occupation and region is derived by multiplying each element of the off-site labor cost matrix by its respective shadow factor.

$$\underline{T_1^S} = O^S \, op. \, T_1^S. \tag{9}[5]$$

---

[5] The symbol *op.* denotes the special matrix operation where, given two rectangular matrices of equal dimensions, for example A and B with elements a_{ij} and b_{ij}, then the the i,jth element of A *op.* B is defined as $a_{ij}b_{ij}$.

Shadow on-site labor cost by occupation and region is derived by multiplying each element of on-site labor cost matrix by its respective shadow factor.

$$\underline{T_2^S} = P^S \ op. \ \underline{T_2^S}. \tag{10}$$

Total shadow labor cost by occupation and region is the matrix sum of the off-site and on-site matrices.

$$\underline{T_*^S} = \underline{T_1^S} + \underline{T_2^S}. \tag{11}$$

Total shadow labor cost is the sum of all of the elements of the matrix derived in equation 11 symbolized by the quadratic form below:

$$\sigma = u \cdot \underline{T_*^S} \cdot [1]. \tag{12}$$

The social cost of the total contract is a similar expression to equation 5 where the difference is in the assessment of the total shadow labor cost.

$$\Delta = \left(\frac{\sigma + u(\underline{r_1} + \underline{p_1} + \underline{c_1})}{ut_* + u(r_1 + p_1 + c_1)} \right) \cdot f. \tag{13}$$

SUPPLEMENTARY ESTIMATES OF NATIONAL AND REGIONAL SECTORAL IMPACT

A NUMBER OF DETAILS on our occupational and industrial estimates which are supplementary to those in Chapters II and III are presented in the six tables in this appendix.

In Table 10A–1 the gross output required from each industry to satisfy a final demand of $1,000 from each of the project types and the gross national product vector are shown. This table complements Table 7 in the text by placing all of the expenditure types on a comparable basis. It will be noted that in Table 7 the gross output figures by industry are not directly comparable because of the variation in the total final demands when summed across industries. In this appendix table, the percentage breakdown of these demands are presented for both the water resource projects and the gross national product. The column of data representing gross output per $1,000 of gross national product can be treated as a capsule picture of the structure of the economy at the time these projects were constructed.

The most striking thing about the data in this table is the substantial disparity between the structure of the economy and the structure of output demands which project construction imposes upon the economy. For example, while about 20 per cent of the economy's production occurs in the broad category of durable goods manufacture, nine of the twelve types of project require over 40 per cent of their gross output demands to be satisfied from this sector. In individual industries, this pattern is even more extreme. Less than 1 per cent of the economy's gross output occurs in the construction machinery industry. In nine of the twelve project types, over 4 per cent of the gross output requirements are drawn from that industry. In one project type (small earth fill dams), construction machinery accounts for 13 per cent of the gross output requirements. Or again, while 1 per cent of the economy's gross output is represented by the stone, clay, and glass products industry, as much as 10 per cent of the gross output requirements for project construction is drawn from this industry. Whereas 2 per cent of the economy's gross output is in mining (including crude petroleum), as much as 26 per cent of gross output requirements for water resource project construction is for extractive products, with most of the project types requiring between 5 and 10 per cent of their gross outputs from this sector.

In contrast, while 6 per cent of the economy's output comes from agriculture, forestry, and fisheries, only one project type requires more than 1 per cent of its gross output demands from this sector, and that type—pile dikes—only requires 2 per cent. The service industries present the same pattern. While nearly 30 per cent of the value of the economy's gross output occurs in these sectors, only about one-half of this percentage is required to fulfill the relative final demands levied on the economy by the construction of water resource projects.

Tables 10A–2 and 10A–3 present figures showing the impact of project construction on detailed occupational and industrial categories. In Table 10A–2, the ten detailed industries for each project type which received the largest output demands are isolated and ranked. Of the twenty-one sectors listed, four are among the top ten industries for each of the project types. They are: primary iron and steel manufacturing; construction, mining, and oilfield equipment; transportation and warehousing; and wholesale and retail trade. In addition, the real estate and rentals sector is among the top ten in ten of the twelve project types and the petroleum refining industry is among the top ten in nine of the project types. In each of the twelve project types, the combined impact on the top ten industries is over 60 per cent of the total gross impact levied on the entire economy. The concentration of demands among industries, noted earlier, is again borne out by this observation. Indeed, whereas each of the project types requires at least 60 per cent of its gross requirements from but ten of the twenty-one detailed industries shown in Table 10A–2, the gross output of the entire group of twenty-one sectors accounts for only a little over 40 per cent of the nation's total gross output.

In Table 10A–3, the more detailed occupational impacts are shown. Here the ten detailed occupations (out of the 156 occupations included in the analysis) receiving the greatest income payments in each type of project are listed and ranked within each type. Again, a few characteristics are noteworthy. First, with only one exception, the occupational demands are extremely concentrated: in all project types except one—powerhouse construction—over 60 per cent of the total labor cost is contained in 10 of the 156 occupations. Indeed, in six of the twelve project types, over 70 per cent of total labor cost is attributable to the top ten occupational classifications. Second, there are certain occupational groups which are major input suppliers to nearly all of the project types. Three catch-all residual categories (managers, officials, and proprietors, not elsewhere classified; clerical and kindred workers, NEC; and operatives and kindred workers, NEC) are among these ubiquitous categories, and the category of labor foremen is a fourth. In addition, the truck and tractor drivers and the excavating and grading machinery operators are ranked among the top ten occupational categories in ten of the twelve project types.

Tables 10A–4, 10A–5, and 10A–6 present some additional results from the calculation of regional sectoral impact. In Table 10A–4, the regional allocation of *total* gross output is displayed for both the large multiple-purpose project and the gross national product final demand vector as the location in which the demands are assumed to be imposed is shifted among regions. In addition, the allocation of the total labor cost of the project is shown. Many of the general patterns noted in Chapter IV are spotlighted here. In particular, the importance of the Mid-Atlantic region (II) and the East North Central region (III) in supplying the generated gross output, irrespective of the region of demand imposition, should be noted. For the water resource project final-demand vector, Region II supplies over $170 (17 per cent) of total output in all except two cases. Similarly, with one exception, Region III supplies over $240 (24 per cent) of gross output. For the GNP final-demand vector, the proportion of gross output supplied by these two regions is smaller but still substantial. For this vector, Region II supplies around 12 per cent in all cases except one, and Region III supplies 15 per cent to 16 per cent with but one exception. This pattern contrasts with the demand imposed on the remaining regions. In both of the expenditure categories, none of these regions supplies in excess of 7 per cent of gross output when demand is imposed outside the region. The data in the column for total labor cost for the projects show this same point. The Mid-Atlantic and East North Central regions, respectively, account for at least $44 and $65 of labor cost in every case except one in which they are not the project region. But no other region accounts for more than $18 of labor cost as project construction is assumed to be shifted among the other regions.

However, while Regions II and III are important suppliers in both expenditure patterns, the smaller impact on these regions from the GNP vector when it is assumed to be imposed in other regions should be noted. No matter where the demand is imposed, the impact of the GNP vector on Regions II and III is smaller than the impact of the water resource project. Again the reason for this pattern is explained in two ways: First is the large proportion of durable goods demand for the water resource project vector and the concentration of the suppliers of these commodities in Regions II and III. Second is the larger proportion of nondurable goods and service demands of the GNP vector and the tendency of these commodities to be locally supplied. No matter in which region the GNP final demand is imposed, there is a larger impact on that region than from the imposition of the final demand of the water resource project. An extreme example of the smaller local impact of the water project is noted in Region VII. When the water project is assumed constructed in this Kentucky-Tennessee region, the local regional output demand is $266 compared with $270 of demand exported to Region III.

For the GNP vector these dollar figures in Region VII are $431 and $164 in Region III.

Whereas Table 10A–4 focuses on the gross output retained in a region as project construction is assumed to occur in one of its constituent states, Table 10A–5 shows how that portion of the gross output not retained in the region in which the demand is imposed is distributed among the remaining regions. Not unexpectedly, Regions II and III again appear as substantial suppliers of gross output in all of the project types. In no case do these two regions taken together supply less than 44 per cent of the output not retained in the project region. In the case of powerhouse construction, their combined output is nearly 70 per cent of the total gross output generated. Although in each of the project types a large portion of the gross outputs that are not retained flows toward the Mid-Atlantic and East North Central regions, there exist substantial variations in the regional allocation among expenditure types. While Region VIII supplies 23 per cent of the nonretained gross output generated by the construction of levees, Region II supplies 17 per cent. In the case of powerhouse construction, however, Region II supplies 28 per cent while Region VIII supplies only 4 per cent. This variation is summarized in the column showing the range of percentages supplied by individual regions as the final-demand vector imposed on Region IV changes. As compared to the final demands for water projects, the GNP vector generally favors Regions II and III less than the capital-intensive projects and tends to distribute its nonretained output toward Regions IV, V, and VII to a larger extent than the water resource projects.

The impact on industries in the durable goods manufacturing category from the construction of the large multiple-purpose project in each of the ten regions is shown in Table 10A–6. No matter where the project is constructed outside of Regions II and III, the durable goods output demanded from each of these two regions greatly exceeds the demand for durable goods in the region where the project is constructed. This is true in spite of the significant emphasis given the project region via the regional preference functions.

Table 10A-1. Twelve Project Types: Gross Output Required to Yield $1,000 of Final Demands, by Industry[a] (in dollars per $1,000 of final demand and per cent of total gross output)

Industry	1958 U.S. gross output		Large earth fill dams		Small earth fill dams		Local flood protection	
	$	%	$	%	$	%	$	%
Agriculture, forestry, & fisheries	118	6	18	1	19	1	19	1
Mining, including crude petroleum	41	2	114	5	135	6	161	8
Construction[b]	117	6	17	1	18	1	20	1
Nondurable goods manufacturing[c]	405	20	350	16	362	17	224	11
Durable goods manufacturing	428	21	964	45	911	43	956	47
Lumber & wood products	31	2	28	1	20	1	41	2
Stone, clay, & glass products	22	1	44	2	35	2	174	8
Primary metals	66	3	169	8	160	6	186	9
Fabricated metals	46	2	159	7	101	5	298	15
Nonelectrical machinery, except construction	49	2	90	4	91	4	51	2
Construction machinery	7	*	210	10	271	13	94	5
Electrical machinery	48	2	30	1	27	1	23	1
Transportation equipment	100	5	225	11	199	9	79	4
Miscellaneous	62	3	9	*	8	*	8	*
Transportation & warehousing	76	4	90	4	112	5	141	7
Wholesale & retail trade	212	11	274	13	252	12	223	11
Services	581	29	312	15	301	14	307	15
Total gross output[d]	1,978		2,140		2,110		2,053	

Asterisk (*) means less than .5 per cent but greater than zero.

[a] Gross output figures in this table are directly proportional to the gross output figures of text Table 7 by project. In this table, dollar values may be compared across the rows because final demand for materials, equipment, and supplies is assumed to be $1,000 for each project.

Pile dikes		Levees		Revet-ments		Power-house construc-tion		Medium concrete dams		Lock & concrete dams		Large multiple-purpose projects		Dredg-ing		Miscel-laneous	
$	%	$	%	$	%	$	%	$	%	$	%	$	%	$	%	$	%
34	2	15	1	24	1	16	1	17	1	16	1	16	1	16	1	24	1
292	15	320	16	480	26	52	2	72	3	163	8	149	7	157	7	167	8
22	1	22	1	26	1	14	1	19	1	18	1	17	1	18	1	18	1
239	12	377	19	202	11	139	7	191	9	175	9	200	10	385	18	377	18
676	34	560	28	357	20	1,373	65	1,141	55	1,025	51	1,049	51	986	45	834	40
152	8	11	1	92	5	28	1	23	1	17	1	25	1	23	1	55	3
26	1	24	1	36	2	36	2	216	10	209	10	152	7	16	1	118	6
104	5	104	5	56	3	234	11	252	12	254	13	252	12	278	13	181	9
62	3	59	3	31	2	97	5	206	10	114	6	194	9	105	5	48	2
59	3	53	3	28	2	426	20	153	7	142	7	146	7	61	3	70	3
131	7	198	10	51	3	46	2	173	8	171	8	101	5	80	4	196	9
18	1	17	1	11	1	443	21	34	2	51	3	125	6	32	1	19	1
119	6	88	4	49	3	46	2	75	4	59	3	39	2	383	18	138	7
6	*	6	*	4	*	17	1	10	*	9	*	14	1	8	*	8	*
225	11	194	10	321	17	80	4	101	5	150	7	141	7	106	5	125	6
188	9	190	9	154	8	174	8	220	11	199	10	181	9	187	9	235	11
312	16	337	17	304	16	252	12	327	16	277	14	296	14	322	15	309	15
1,990		2,015		1,868		2,099		2,088		2,023		2,049		2,177		2,089	

[b] Refers only to maintenance and repair construction. In the 1958 input-output study, new construction is treated as a final demand.

[c] In all of the project types, the overwhelming supplier in the nondurable goods sector is petroleum and related products.

[d] Columns may not add because of rounding.

Table 10A–2. Gross Output Required from Top Ten Input-Output Industries to Yield Final Demand, by Project Type (in dollars per $1,000 of total contract cost and per cent of total gross output)

Input-output numbers and industries	Per cent of total U.S. gross output	Large earth fill dams			Small earth fill dams			Local flood protection			Pile dikes			Levees			Revetments		
		Rank	$	%	Rank	$	%	Rank	$	%	Rank	$	%	Rank	$	%	Rank	$	%
8 Crude petroleum & natural gas	1.2	8	46	4.0	8	41	3.2							6	50	6.1	6	39	2.8
9 Stone & clay mining & quarrying	.2							7	47	4.6				5	74	9.0	1	308	22.3
20 Lumber & wood products, except containers	1.0	9	34	3.0	6	72	5.7				1	124	11.5				5	67	4.8
27 Chemicals & selected chemical products	1.3	4	85	7.4	5	75	5.9				4	81	7.5						
31 Petroleum refining & related industries	2.0							8	38	3.7	9	29	2.7	1	93	11.3	4	72	5.2
36 Stone & clay products	.9							3	86	8.3	6	47	4.4						
37 Primary iron & steel manufacturing	2.2	5	71	6.2	4	78	6.1	5	71	6.9				7	35	4.2	9	31	2.2
38 Primary nonferrous metal manufacturing	1.1	6	56	4.9	9	32	2.5				7	46	4.3						
40 Heating, plumbing & structural metal products	.9							1	118	11.5									
42 Other fabricated metal products	.7																		
43 Engines & turbines	.3																		
45 Construction, mining & oil field machinery	.4	3	112	9.8	1	163	12.8	6	47	4.6	5	71	6.6	2	81	9.8	8	37	2.7
46 Materials handling machinery & equipment	.1																		
53 Electric industrial equipment & apparatus	.6																		
59 Motor vehicles & equipment	2.6	2	116	10.2	3	115	9.0	9	36	3.5				10	19	2.3			
61 Other transportation equipment	.4																		
65 Transportation & warehousing	3.8	7	48	4.2	7	68	5.3	4	71	6.9	8	43	4.0	3	79	9.6	2	238	17.2
68 Electric, gas, water & sanitary services	2.3										2	122	11.3						
69 Wholesale & retail trade	10.7	1	146	12.8	2	152	11.9	2	112	10.9	3	102	9.4	4	78	9.5	3	114	8.2
70 Finance & insurance	3.0													9	21	2.5	10	30	2.2
71 Real estate & rental	7.0	10	29	2.5	10	31	2.4	10	25	2.4	10	28	2.6	8	26	3.2	7	39	2.8
Column total[a]	42.7		743	65.1		827	65.0		651	63.2		693	64.2		556	67.5		975	70.5
Other production sectors			398	34.9		446	35.0		379	36.8		387	35.8		268	32.5		408	29.5
Total gross output			1,141	100		1,273	100		1,030	100		1,080	100		824	100		1,383	100

a Columns may not add because of rounding.

Table 10A–2. (Continued)

Input-output numbers and industries	Powerhouse construction			Medium concrete dams			Lock & concrete dams			Large multiple-purpose projects			Dredging			Miscellaneous		
	Rank	$	%	Rank	$	%	Rank	$	%	Rank	$	%	Rank	$	%	Rank	$	%
8 Crude petroleum & natural gas							6	77	5.3	8	47	4.5	5	55	5.6	8	56	4.5
9 Stone & clay mining & quarrying																		
20 Lumber & wood products, except containers																		
27 Chemicals & selected chemical products													9	29	2.9	9	46	3.7
31 Petroleum refining & related industries							9	32	2.2				3	103	10.4	3	104	8.3
36 Stone & clay products	4	113	6.6	2	113	10.1	2	149	10.2	3	77	7.3				7	69	5.5
37 Primary iron & steel manufacturing	5	76	4.5	3	105	9.4	1	157	10.7	1	100	9.5	2	109	11.1	4	95	7.6
38 Primary nonferrous metal manufacturing				9	29	2.6				10	30	2.8						
40 Heating, plumbing & structural metal products	10	32	1.9	5	84	7.5	7	50	3.4	4	75	7.1						
42 Other fabricated metal products													8	32	3.2			
43 Engines & turbines	2	247	14.5	4	92	8.3	4	123	8.4	9	40	3.8						
45 Construction, mining & oil field machinery	8	37	2.2	10	27	2.4	8	33	2.3	7	52	4.9	7	36	3.7	2	117	9.4
46 Materials handling machinery & equipment	9	33	1.9															
53 Electric industrial equipment & apparatus	1	322	18.9							6	54	5.1						
59 Motor vehicles & equipment				8	31	2.8										5	77	6.2
61 Other transportation equipment				6	54	4.8	5	109	7.5	5	72	6.8	1	162	16.4			
65 Transportation & warehousing	6	65	3.8	7	37	3.3							6	48	4.9	6	75	6.0
68 Electric, gas, water & sanitary services																		
69 Wholesale & retail trade	3	142	8.3	1	117	10.5	3	144	9.8	2	93	8.8	4	85	8.6	1	140	11.2
70 Finance & insurance																		
71 Real estate & rental	7	39	2.3				10	32	2.2				10	26	2.6	10	32	2.6
Column total[a]		1,106	65.0		689	61.8		906	61.9		640	60.7		685	69.5		811	65.1
Other production sectors		595	35.0		425	38.2		557	38.1		414	39.3		301	30.5		435	34.9
Total gross output		1,701	100		1,114	100		1,463	100		1,054	100		986	100		1,246	100

Table 10A–3. Total Labor Cost Allocated to Top Ten Detailed Occupations, by Project Type (in dollars per $1,000 of total contract cost and per cent of total labor cost)

Occupation-industry matrix numbers and detailed occupational category	Large earth fill dams			Small earth fill dams			Local flood protection			Pile dikes			Levees			Revetments		
	Rank	$	%	Rank	$	%	Rank	$	%	Rank	$	%	Rank	$	%	Rank	$	%
10 Other engineers, NEC	10	21	3.4							10	21	3.5	9	21	3.6			
55 Managers, officials, & proprietors, NEC	1	59	9.7	2	73	11.0	3	60	9.0	2	64	10.7	3	54	9.4	2	65	12.6
57 Officers, pilots, ship engineers																		
69 Clerical & kindred workers, NEC	8	31	5.1	6	32	4.8	9	27	4.0	7	25	4.2	8	22	3.8	6	30	6.0
70 Sales workers				9	14	2.1												
71 Carpenters				10	11	1.7	6	48	7.2									
74 Electricians																		
75 Excavating, grading, machine operators	5	49	8.1	1	131	19.8	2	67	10.0	1	74	12.3	1	89	15.5	8	22	4.3
80 Structural metal workers							8	29	4.3									
81 Foremen, NEC	7	32	5.3	5	39	5.9	7	41	6.1	8	23	3.8	10	20	3.5	9	21	4.1
97 Motor vehicle mechanics	9	23	3.8	7	26	3.9							7	31	5.4			
114 Cranemen, derrickmen, hoistmen																		
117 Other inspectors, NEC	6	41	6.7				10	18	2.7	6	41	6.8	6	41	7.1	10	12	2.3
124 Craftsmen & kindred workers, NEC																		
131 Welders & flame cutters																		
134 Drivers, bus, truck, tractor	2	59	9.7	8	21	3.2	5	51	7.6	5	51	8.5	2	65	11.3	5	36	7.0
138 Sailors & deck hands										9	21	3.5				7	22	4.3
143 Mine operatives, laborers, NEC																3	42	8.1
146 Operatives & kindred workers, NEC	3	56	9.2	3	71	10.7	4	56	8.4	4	51	8.5	4	53	9.2	4	42	8.1
151 Cooks, except private household																		
155 Laborers, except farm	4	55	9.0	4	57	8.6	1	89	13.3	3	60	10.0	5	46	8.0	1	66	12.8
Column total[a]		425	69.4		475	71.8		486	72.9		432	72.0		442	76.7		358	69.2
Other occupations		187	30.6		187	28.2		181	27.1		168	28.0		134	23.3		159	30.8
Total labor cost[a]		612	100		662	100		667	100		600	100		576	100		517	100

NEC means not elsewhere classified.
[a] Columns may not add because of rounding.

Table 10A–3. (Continued)

Occupation-industry matrix numbers and detailed occupational category	Powerhouse construction			Medium concrete dams			Lock & concrete dams			Large multiple-purpose projects			Dredging			Miscellaneous		
	Rank	$	%	Rank	$	%	Rank	$	%	Rank	$	%	Rank	$	%	Rank	$	%
10 Other engineers, NEC	1	83	12.0	10	21	3.1							8	21	3.4	8	21	3.5
55 Managers, officials, & proprietors, NEC				2	62	9.2	1	77	11.2	2	64	8.9	5	44	7.1	2	65	10.7
57 Officers, pilots, ship engineers	3	48	6.9	8	29	4.3	6	37	5.4				1	95	15.3			
69 Clerical & kindred workers, NEC	10	16	2.3							8	30	4.2	7	24	3.9	7	33	5.5
70 Sales workers																		
71 Carpenters	6	29	4.2	6	32	4.7	8	31	4.5	6	49	6.8						
74 Electricians	7	21	3.0							9	26	3.6						
75 Excavating, grading, machine operators				7	30	4.5	7	35	5.1	7	37	5.1				3	57	9.4
80 Structural metal workers										10	22	3.1						
81 Foremen, NEC	5	39	5.6	5	38	5.6	5	42	6.1	3	58	8.1	10	17	2.7	10	17	2.8
97 Motor vehicle mechanics							10	17	2.5							9	20	3.3
114 Cranemen, derrickmen, hoistmen							9	18	2.6									
117 Other inspectors, NEC	9	16	2.3	4	41	6.1							6	41	6.6	6	41	6.8
124 Craftsmen & kindred workers, NEC										5	53	7.4						
131 Welders & flame cutters													9	18	2.9			
134 Drivers, bus, truck, tractor	8	17	2.5	9	28	4.2	4	47	6.9							4	56	9.3
138 Sailors & deck hands													3	68	11.0			
143 Mine operatives, laborers, NEC	2	74	10.7	3	57	8.5	2	68	9.9									
146 Operatives & kindred workers, NEC										4	57	7.9	2	70	11.3	1	68	11.2
151 Cooks, except private household																		
155 Laborers, except farm	4	41	5.9	1	87	12.9	3	58	8.5	1	89	12.4	4	54	8.7	5	51	8.4
Column total		382	55.3		426	63.2		430	62.8		485	67.5		451	72.6		430	71.1
Other occupations		309	44.7		248	36.8		255	37.2		234	32.5		170	27.4		175	28.9
Total labor cost[a]		691	100		674	100		685	100		719	100		621	100		605	100

Table 10A–4. Total Gross Output Required from Each of Ten Regions when the Final Demands of the Large Multiple-Purpose Project and Gross National Product[a] Are Imposed on Each of the Regions, and Total Project Labor Cost (in dollars per $1,000 of total contract cost)

Region upon which demands are imposed	I New England			II Mid-Atlantic			III East North Central			IV West North Central			V Southeast		
	Gross output		Labor cost	Gross output		Labor cost	Gross output		Labor cost	Gross output		Labor cost	Gross output		Labor cost
	Project	GNP		Project	GNP		Project	GNP		Project	GNP		Project	GNP	
I New England	326	472	534	33	29	9	28	30	8	44	37	12	45	37	12
II Mid-Atlantic	172	118	46	599	632	608	102	93	26	172	118	46	175	119	46
III East North Central	257	157	68	189	131	49	724	675	645	255	153	68	262	159	90
IV West North Central	45	54	12	33	46	8	27	43	6	335	504	538	44	53	12
V Southeast	36	50	10	26	42	7	23	44	6	35	49	9	313	488	533
VI Lower Atlantic	32	26	9	24	21	6	22	22	6	31	26	8	32	25	8
VII Kentucky-Tennessee	16	17	4	12	13	3	10	14	3	15	16	4	16	15	4
VIII West South Central	61	54	13	50	48	10	40	46	7	59	51	12	60	53	13
IX Mountain	24	19	6	20	17	4	18	16	4	23	17	5	23	18	5
X West Coast	64	64	17	47	53	13	40	51	10	62	61	17	63	64	17
Total[b]	1,032	1,032	719	1,032	1,032	719	1,032	1,032	719	1,032	1,032	719	1,032	1,032	719

[a] For the meaning of the data in the GNP columns and their relationship to the project data, see footnotes 13 and 14 of Chapter III.
[b] Columns may not add because of rounding.

Table 10A–4. (Continued)

Region upon which demands are imposed	VI Lower Atlantic Gross output Project	GNP	Labor cost	VII Kentucky-Tennessee Gross output Project	GNP	Labor cost	VIII West South Central Gross output Project	GNP	Labor cost	IX Mountain Gross output Project	GNP	Labor cost	X West Coast Gross output Project	GNP	Labor cost
						Region in which project is assumed to be constructed								
I New England	45	39	12	46	39	13	45	38	12	46	40	13	42	36	12
II Mid-Atlantic	177	123	47	181	126	48	173	122	46	182	128	49	166	115	44
III East North Central	264	162	70	270	164	72	253	158	67	270	165	72	247	150	65
IV West North Central	45	56	12	46	56	10	43	53	11	46	56	12	42	50	11
V Southeast	36	49	10	37	50	10	35	50	9	37	52	10	33	49	9
VI Lower Atlantic	**300**	**450**	**527**	33	26	9	31	27	8	33	28	9	30	24	8
VII Kentucky-Tennessee	16	16	4	**266**	**431**	**522**	15	17	4	16	17	4	15	16	4
VIII West South Central	61	54	13	62	55	13	**353**	**487**	**538**	62	55	13	56	50	12
IX Mountain	24	19	6	24	19	6	23	18	5	**274**	**426**	**522**	22	17	5
X West Coast	65	65	18	66	66	18	61	63	17	66	66	18	**379**	**525**	**552**
Total[b]	1,032	1,032	719	1,032	1,032	719	1,032	1,032	719	1,032	1,032	719	1,032	1,032	719

Table 10A–5. Regional Allocation of Gross Output Not Retained in the Region of Project Location when the Final Demands of the Twelve Project Types and Gross National Product Are Imposed in the Lower Atlantic Region (in per cent of gross output not retained)

	Region	Large earth fill dams	Small earth fill dams	Local flood protection	Pile dikes	Levees	Revetments
I	New England	4	4	5	6	4	5
II	Mid-Atlantic	18	18	22	17	17	17
III	East North Central	39	40	35	31	33	27
IV	West North Central	6	6	6	6	6	6
V	Southeast	4	4	6	6	4	6
VI	Lower Atlantic	–	–	–	–	–	–
VII	Kentucky-Tennessee	2	2	2	2	2	2
VIII	West South Central	15	14	11	14	23	18
IX	Mountain	3	3	3	4	4	4
X	West Coast	9	8	10	14	9	14
Total[b]		100	100	100	100	100	100

[a] For the meaning of the data in the columns giving gross output from GNP and their relationship to the project data, see footnote 13 of Chapter III.

[b] Columns may not add because of rounding.

Power-house construc-tion	Medium concrete dams	Lock & concrete dams	Large multiple-purpose projects	Dredging	Miscel-laneous	Gross output from GNP[a]	Range	Median
8	5	5	6	6	4	7	4–8	5
28	22	22	24	21	18	21	17–28	18
40	37	37	36	29	36	28	27–40	35
5	7	7	6	5	6	10	5–10	6
3	5	5	5	5	5	8	3–8	5
–	–	–	–	–	–	–	–	–
2	2	2	2	2	1	3	1–3	2
4	9	9	8	18	17	9	4–23	11
3	3	3	3	3	3	3	3–4	3
8	9	7	9	10	10	11	7–14	9
100	100	100	100	100	100	100		

Table 10A–6. Total Gross Output of Durable Goods Required from Each of Ten Regions when the Large Multiple-Purpose Project Is Constructed in Each of the Regions (in dollars per $1,000 of total contract cost)

Region upon which demands are imposed	Region in which project is assumed to be constructed									
	I New England	II Mid-Atlantic	III East North Central	IV West North Central	V Southeast	VI Lower Atlantic	VII Kentucky-Tennessee	VIII West South Central	IX Mountain	X West Coast
I New England	**73**	21	17	30	30	31	32	31	32	29
II Mid-Atlantic	122	**278**	65	122	124	126	129	124	130	117
III East North Central	191	135	**379**	189	195	197	201	189	201	183
IV West North Central	27	17	12	**76**	26	27	28	26	28	24
V Southeast	20	13	10	19	**58**	20	21	20	21	18
VI Lower Atlantic	19	12	11	18	18	**49**	19	18	19	17
VII Kentucky-Tennessee	8	5	4	8	8	9	**26**	8	9	8
VIII West South Central	25	18	10	23	24	25	26	**70**	26	22
IX Mountain	13	10	8	12	12	13	13	12	**30**	12
X West Coast	42	30	23	41	41	43	44	41	44	**110**
Total[a]	539	539	539	539	539	539	539	539	539	539

[a] Columns may not add because of rounding.

INDEX

Alterman, Jack, 16n
Appalachia, 2, 8, 25, 87
Army Corps of Engineers, 15, 18, 19n, 23n, 24

Benefit-cost investment criteria for water-resource projects: dependence on demand and employment data, 3; underutilization of crafts and skills significant for, 10; assumption of full vs. less than full employment in, 87, 92
Benefit/cost ratios computed for projects: divergence of "nominal" costs from opportunity-cost ratios, 92; relation of adjusted real to nominal B/C ratios, 93–94
BLS. *See* Labor Statistics, Bureau of
Bureaus. *See other part of title.*
Business Economics, Office of (Department of Commerce), 22, 23, 25, 26n, 41n, 116
Business taxes. *See* Indirect business taxes

Capital: rate of return regarded as lost in idle capacity period, 4; a primary factor in the opportunity cost of resource use, 65; equilibrium price of defined, 66; alternative use of required units of, 67; divergence between real and nominal costs of, 91
Capital consumption allowances (depreciation): in expenditure for a final good, 17; as a true social cost in a fully employed economy, 68, 69
Capital intensity of expenditures: significance of for changing the ranking of alternatives under conditions of less than full employment, 93, 94
Capital response functions, 70–75
Capital shadow factors (by industry), 75, 78, 118n, 135–36
Census, Bureau of the (Department of Commerce), 9n, 27n, 42n, 75n, 81n
Clark, J. M., 65n
Computer methodology for sectoral demand models, 113, 124
Contractors' tax payments: as a proportion of total contract cost, 19

Control Data Corporation, 115
Corporate profits: generated by expenditure for a final good, 17; as a proportion of total contract cost, 19; components of, 26n; as a true social cost in a fully employed economy, 68, 69
Cost adjustments for public investments: under conditions of less than full employment, 65, 66, 87; regional requirements for in different project types, 81, 83; importance of for a choice among alternatives, 94–95
Cost-benefit analysis. *See under Benefit-cost entries.*
Creamer, Daniel, 128n, 131n

Data compilations for the national sectoral model: sources for data, 18, 19n, 22–27 *passim*; primary expenditure data, 22–25
—bills of final demand: defined, 22; variability in industrial-demands pattern among project types, 23–24; final-output demands from transportation equipment, construction machinery, and mining industries, 24; demands on transportation services and trade sectors, 24
—data inputs intrinsic to the model: input-output coefficients pertaining to interindustry relations, occupational composition, and value-added components, 18, 25–27; ratio of each value-added component to gross output for each industry, 25–26, 98, 99; occupational labor coefficients for each industry, 26–27, 99; breakdown of off-site man-year requirements for each project type, 27; gross output figures emerging from the input-output computation, 27n
—data inputs peculiar to the final expenditure: material, equipment, and supply inputs and on-site employee compensation payments, 18; variance in the structure of inputs seen in the ratios of material, equipment, and supply costs to on-site labor costs, 19, 22n; use of "purchaser value" and

153

capacity, 67; estimates of for *1960*, 80

Overhead: as a proportion of total contract cost, 19, 98

Peacock, Alan T., 2*n*

Phillips, Almarin, 10*n*, 131*n*

Prest, A. R., 1*n*

Price inflexibility: assumption of in the shift from the fully employed to the less than fully employed economy, 67*n*

Production factors: identification of, 67; opportunity returns foregone in diverting fully employed factors, 68

Project-construction site: differences in cost adjustment for a project type resulting from a shift in location among regions, 81, 83, 85, 86

Proprietor and rental income: generated by expenditure for a final good, 17; components of, 26*n*; in the mining, wholesale and retail trade, and service sectors, 35; as a true social cost in a fully employed economy, 68, 69; in costs adjustment to total contract cost, 79

Public expenditure criteria: assumption of full employment in, 1, 3; consideration of opportunity costs during construction period and income and employment after construction, 12–13; alternative outputs in a fully employed and in a less than fully employed economy, 66, 67, 68, 69. *See also* Models of the economy; Public investment

Public investment: need of costs adjustment in evaluation of, 3. *See also* Opportunity costs of public investment; Social cost of public investment in water-resource facilities; Water-resource investment

Real costs: estimates of as a percentage of money costs, 73; divergence between nominal costs and, 94

Reclamation, Bureau of (Department of the Interior), 15, 18

Regional distribution coefficients for the national industries: input-output sectors and, 126–27

Regional gross output, 140, 141

Regional sectoral demand model: output-transportability and consumption features of, 38; states included in each of ten regions used in, 43

—formal model: computation procedure for, 41–42; mathematical consistency of national and regional models, 42*n*, 112–14; mathematical formulation of, 106–11; analysis by the computer process, 119–22

—groups of industries presented according to spatial points of production and consumption: definition of Types A, B, C, and Local, and allocation of outputs, 38–42, 110–11

—input-output coefficients: output of national industries in each region, 42, 126–27; "final" output requirements for Local-to-national and Local-to-Local industry, 112–13, 113–14; national and regional analyses, facing 124

—regional preference functions: degree of dependence on productive capacity, 39; assumed to be complete for Local type, 40; for Types B and C, 40–41, 42*n*, 110

Regional sectoral impact of public project construction: limitations on precision in analysis of, 37; demands and regional impact of the multiple-purpose project, 43, 44, 46, 48–59 *passim*, 148–49

—durable goods industries: as input suppliers to the larger projects, 48, 51, 56, 57, 152; regional distributions for, compared with nondurable goods, 49; share of output retained in regions, 57; output required from each region for multiple-purpose projects, 152

—GNP final-demand vector: composition of, 43*n*; comparison of regional distribution of demands of gross output and, 43, 48–60 *passim*; characteristics of, 64

—gross output: allocation of to the region of project location, by industry, 52, 54–55; disparity among regions in the ability to retain outputs, 56; requirement from each region on which demands are imposed, 148–49; regional allocation of output not retained in the region of project location, 150–51

—industrial gross output demands: estimates for major production sectors yielded by model, 43, 142–43, 144–45; disparity among individual industry outputs retained in a region, 56

—labor cost: allocation of to the region of project location, by occupation, 53; divergences among regions, 56–57; on-site labor cost components re-

U.S. Census of Population: unemployment rates by occupational groups for the United States compared with selected geographic areas, 8; data on wages and salaries (*1960* Census), 27

U.S. Council of Economic Advisors, 73*n*

Vaccara, Beatrice N., 22*n*, 25*n*, 26*n*

Water-resource investment: need of evaluation with adjustment for market and opportunity costs, 3; output and employment generated by, 91. *See also* Benefit-cost investment criteria for water-resource projects

Water-resource public development projects: construction categories of, 6; potential source of on-site labor for depressed areas, 25; high employment ratio per dollar of expenditure in, 88; industrial demands imposed by, 88; labor demands imposed by, 89, 90; gross output demands imposed on regions, 89–90; project names and locations, 100–101. *See also* Data compilations for the national sectoral model; Expenditure categories for project construction

West Coast region (X), 46, 50, 55, 56, 60, 61, 62, 126–27, 148–49, 150–51, 152

West North Central region (IV), 44, 55, 60, 62, 83, 126–27, 141, 148–49, 150–51, 152

West South Central region (VIII), 46, 48, 55, 56, 60, 62, 85, 126–27, 141, 148–49, 150–51, 152

West Virginia, 8, 9, 10, 43, 89

Wharton School of Finance and Commerce: Economics Research Unit's estimates on utilization of industrial capacity (*1947–65*), 11–12, 128, 129